What We Believe

Helping children understand the beliefs of the Seventh-day Adventist Church

Jerry D. Thomas

Teaching Tips by
Jerry and Kitty Thomas

Pacific Press® Publishing Association

Nampa, Idaho
Oshawa, Ontario, Canada
www.pacificpress.com

Cover and book design by **Gerald and Sharon Monks**

Illustration credits:

Paintings, copyright Pacific Press®

Clyde Provonsha – pp. 22, 58, 60, 65
Harry Anderson – pp. 29, 43, 53, 59
Joe Maniscalco – p. 42
John Steel – pp. 18, 19, 20, 21, 26, 28, 49, 61, 63, 64, 66, 67
Lars Justinen – pp. 27, 36, 37, 38, 39, 46, 51, 52, 54, 55
Max Woolley – p. 34
Robert Ayres – p. 12

Photos copyright dreamstime.com – pp. 23, 24, 25, 30, 32, 33, 41, 44, 47, 57
Photos copyright iStockphoto.com – pp. 13, 17, 31, 40, 45, 56, 62

Copyright 2006 by **Pacific Press**® **Publishing Association**
Printed in the United States of America
All rights reserved

ISBN 13: 978-0-8163-2167-4
ISBN 10: 0–8163–2167–1

Additional copies of this book are available by
calling toll-free **1-800-765-6955** or by visiting <**www.adventistbookcenter.com**>.

06 07 08 09 10 • 5 4 3 2 1

Dedication

This book is dedicated to Mrs. Sox—Aileen Andres Sox.
She saw the need to help root our children in the beliefs of our
church and asked me to write about our fundamental beliefs in the pages
of *Primary Treasure*®, demonstrating once again her dedication
to meeting the spiritual needs of our church's children.

Also by
Jerry D. Thomas

Conversations With Jesus

The Detective Zack series

The Great Stories for Kids series

Messiah

The Shoebox Kids series

The Shoebox Kids Bible Stories series

Contents

Preface

This book is intended to help kids understand what their church teaches—to help them understand what it means to be an Adventist. It isn't meant to be comprehensive or complete but is meant to serve as an introduction to and a summary of the twenty-eight Fundamental Beliefs of the Seventh-day Adventist Church.

The Teaching Tips section will assist any teacher, parent, or caregiver who is trying to help children understand the doctrines of their church. By tying these beliefs into a concrete story or experience, we make them more real and more meaningful. By attaching them to experiences that children can identify with, we make them a part of their identity—we make the church a part of their identity.

Use the Teaching Tips with individual children, Sabbath School classes, or Bible lessons in the classroom. Adapt them to meet the needs of the children you are reaching. Every child is unique, and each one will have different questions as they seek to understand.

Some people think of writing this kind of information for children as "dumbing it down." I don't buy that. In making something complex understandable to children, you don't write "dumber." You write more clearly. You use simple words and short sentences. You don't try to tell them everything—you try to tell them the most important things in words they can understand.

Someone has said that you don't really understand a subject fully until you can explain it to a ten-year-old. If you've never really wrapped your mind around some of the teachings of your church, take this opportunity to study them for yourself again.

We Are Adventists

When people ask me what church I go to, I tell them, "I go to the Seventh-day Adventist church." Sometimes they ask, "What do Adventists believe?" That's what we're going to talk about in this book. I hope it helps you understand what your church teaches. And I hope it helps you know what to say if someone ever asks you what church you go to. But most of all, I hope it helps you remember how much God loves you, because that's what these beliefs are all about.

The Bible, the Word of God

Do you have a bookshelf in your room? I do. On my bookshelf, I have many different kinds of books all lined up in a row, books that I like to read. One of the books on that shelf is a Bible.

The Bible is really a whole bookshelf of books all by itself. It has sixty-six books inside. Some are short. Some are long. Some are stories. Some are songs. Some talk about things that happened long ago. Some talk about things that are going to happen in the future.

I believe that the Bible is a long message from God. It's called the Holy Scriptures, or Holy Writings, because all the different things in the sixty-six books tell us about God and His plans for us.

God didn't write the Bible with His own hands. Most of the time, He didn't give the writers words to write—He gave them thoughts to think. Sometimes He helped them remember what happened so they could write the story. Sometimes He helped them find just the right words for a song or a poem about Him. Sometimes He helped them think clearly as they explained His plans. Sometimes He showed them things that were happening far away or things that would happen someday in the future.

Then each one wrote down those thoughts the best they could to explain or tell the story. That's what we mean when we say that the Bible is "inspired" by God.

I believe the Bible gives us the truth about God. It tells us who God is and how He wants to save us. It tells us how God wants us to live. The Bible says, "All Scripture is given by God and is useful for teaching, for showing people what is wrong in their lives, for correcting faults, and for teaching how to live right" (2 Timothy 3:16).

The Bible isn't an encyclopedia. It doesn't tell us everything about science or history. It tells us about God and about His plans for all people.

The Bible is the Word of God because it is how God speaks to us today.

Summary

The Bible is God's book. It is His message to us. In the Bible, we can hear God's voice speaking to us.

Teaching Tips

1. Encourage the children to discuss the different kinds of books on a bookshelf at home or at school, and ask them about their favorite books. Point out that we can learn many different kinds of things from books. Books of stories, poems, pictures, and facts all teach us things. Then apply this point to the Bible—how its many different types of writing teach us many different things about God and His plans.

2. Discuss what our belief that the Bible is "inspired" means. Because children haven't written or created much in their lives, this will be a difficult concept for them. Don't hesitate to describe the Bible's inspiration as a miracle, something God does that we don't completely understand.

3. Point out that while the Bible is never wrong, it doesn't answer every question. Ask several questions about where to find information—for example, where would we go to learn what colors are in a rainbow? And where would we go to find out when the next full moon will be? A science book or encyclopedia would be a good place to find those answers, but not the Bible. Then talk about questions for which the Bible has answers: How much does God love us? What are His plans for us? Where did this world come from?

God Is Three Persons

The grace of the Lord Jesus Christ, the love of God, and the fellowship of the Holy Spirit be with you all.

— 2 Corinthians 13:14

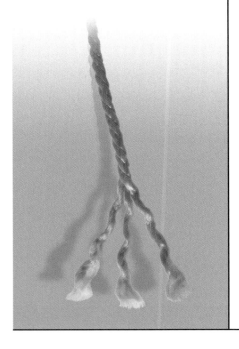

Have you ever used a rope as a lasso? Once, I roped my dog, Brutus. But Brutus was so big that he dragged me in circles until I was tied up in the rope!

While I was lying there on the ground, I saw that my rope was made up of three smaller ropes all wound tightly together. That's what made it strong enough not to break when Brutus was dragging me. Look at the next rope you see—it's probably the same.

I believe that there is only one God in the whole universe. I believe that God has existed forever and that He created everything there is. But when I say God, I'm talking about Three Persons—God the Father; Jesus, who is His Son; and the Holy Spirit. They work together in everything They do, and They all have the same love for everything and everyone. They all love each of us and want us to live forever in heaven with Them.

Just as my one rope was made up of three ropes wound together, our one God is made up of Three Persons who work together. Because They act the same and think the same, we think of Them as one God.

The Three Persons worked together to create the world. They were the Ones who said, "Let us make human beings in our image and likeness" (Genesis 1:26). Jesus named all three of Them when He said, "Go and make followers of all people in the world. Baptize them in the name of the Father and the Son and the Holy Spirit" (Matthew 28:19).

The Bible tells us that God knows everything. He knows everything that has ever happened and everything that will happen. He's so powerful, so wonderful, and so amazing that we can't even imagine what He looks like or what He can do.

But we can know many things about God. He tells us about Himself in the Bible. We can see God best in the story of Jesus. When Jesus helped people, He was showing us what God is like. Most important, Jesus showed us how much God loves each one of us—His human children.

Teaching Tips

1. If you've ever used a rope as a lasso or done some other interesting thing with a rope, share that story with the children.

2. The doctrine of the Trinity isn't simple. People have written whole books to explain it, and Christians have argued about this doctrine for thousands of years. So, don't expect children to understand it completely. The important point here is that the Bible doesn't picture numerous gods warring with each other over human beings. Instead, it teaches that each Person of the Godhead is single-minded about saving us; They're all working together to save us.

3. Try to imagine with the children what the process of Creation was like. Did God the Father and the Holy Spirit laugh when Jesus created giraffes? Did Jesus surprise Them with hippopotamuses? Imagine each Member of the Godhead enjoying the act of creation and talking about how much kids were going to like what They created.

4. This is a good time to help children see that God is so big and complex that we can't understand Him. All we do know is what He's told us in the Bible. But He's not like a stronger, nicer person—He's much more than human. He's some other wonderful kind of Being who loves us.

Summary

God is Three Persons— God the Father; Jesus, who is His Son; and the Holy Spirit. Because They act the same and think the same, we think of Them as one God.

God the Father

"I am the Lord. The Lord is a God who shows mercy, who is kind, who doesn't become angry quickly, who has great love and faithfulness and is kind to thousands of people."

— Exodus 34:6, 7

There is a story about five blind men who were asked to describe an elephant. Because they couldn't see, they each felt the elephant with their hands to find out what it was like.

One man grabbed the elephant's tail. "An elephant is like a rope," he said. Another man felt the elephant's leg. "Oh, an elephant is like a tree trunk," he said. The third man put his hands on the elephant's side. "An elephant is just like a wall," he reported.

The fourth man felt the elephant's ear. "An elephant is like a fan," he said. The fifth man felt the elephant's trunk. "An elephant is like a big hose," he said.

You know what an elephant looks like. Were any of these people right?

Well, yes, they were. An elephant's tail is like a rope. And its legs are as big as tree trunks. But an elephant is more than just a tail or four legs or a trunk. It's a whole big animal.

None of the men were wrong about the elephant. They just didn't know everything.

We have the same problem when we talk about God. We know some things about Him, but we don't know everything. He is greater and more powerful than we can even imagine.

Here are some of the things we know: God is the King of the universe. He has always existed, and He created everything. He keeps all the stars and planets spinning in space. God is holy. He never does anything wrong. He is never selfish. He is always fair, and He always keeps His promises.

When Jesus was baptized in the Jordan River, God the Father was there. He said, "This is My Son, whom I love." Jesus taught us most of what we know about God. Jesus said, "If you've seen Me, you've seen the Father. When I help or heal someone, that's what My Father is like. When I treat people with kindness, that's what My Father is like. And when I become angry because people are mean and selfish, that's what My Father is like too."

John 3:16 tells us, "God loved the world so much that he gave his one and only Son so that whoever believes in him may not be lost, but have eternal life." That's how much God the Father loves us.

Teaching Tips

1. Children will enjoy this game: Place several items in shoeboxes and have the kids try to guess what they are only by feel (no peeking inside). Mix some common things (a sponge, a grape, an orange, a toothbrush) with some items more difficult to identify by feel (an unsharpened pencil, a gummy worm, a cattail or other seedpod, a potato) and let them guess. This will help them understand the difficulty described in the story of the blind men and the elephant, and the difficulty of understanding God.

2. Show the children some pictures of space and stars to help them begin to understand the size of God's universe and how big and powerful He must be.

3. Children love stories about Jesus. The most important thing we can tell them about God the Father is what Jesus told us: If you know Me, you know what My Father is like.

4. Compare how much the children's parents love them with God's love for Jesus. Then point out that God loves us so much that He sent His Child into a dangerous place to save us.

Summary

We don't know everything about God the Father, but we know He loves us because He sent His Son Jesus to save us.

Jesus

"The baby will be holy and will be called the Son of God."

— Luke 1:35

Have you ever seen a bird flying around inside a store? One day I watched a sparrow flying and cheeping and looking for the way out. I wanted to help the bird, so I went to the door and opened it. But the sparrow didn't come to the door and fly out. It just kept flying around near the ceiling. I thought, If I could be a bird for just a few minutes, I could show it how to get outside and be safe.

Jesus thought the same thing when people stopped trusting Him and got trapped in sin. He said, "I will become a human and save them. I will show them the way out." And that's just what He did.

Like God the Father, Jesus has always been alive. It was Jesus who created our world and the people who live here. And even before Adam and Eve sinned, He had a plan to save people and to help them love and trust God again.

As part of His plan, Jesus was born as a human child. Somehow, He became both a human being and God at the same time. Then He grew up and lived just like we do. He was tempted to be selfish and mean, but He was always kind instead. He always treated others with kindness and love. His life shows us how to live that way too.

Jesus did things no one else could do. He walked on water, and He told a storm to be quiet. He took one boy's lunch, and from it He made enough food to feed thousands of people. He healed sick people and blind people and people who were hurt. He even brought dead people back to life!

But part of His plan was to die for us so we could go to heaven and live with Him. When people became angry with Him, He let them arrest Him and nail Him to a cross. That's how He died. But after three days, Jesus came back to life!

Before Jesus returned to heaven, He made this promise: "There are many rooms in my Father's house; I would not tell you this if it were not true. I am going there to prepare a place for you. After I go and prepare a place for you, I will come back and take you to be with me so that you may be where I am" (John 14:2, 3).

Just like His Father, Jesus always keeps His promises, so He is coming back very soon. This time, He will put an end to sin and pain and death. Then He will create the earth again and make everything perfect like it was the first time He created it. And every person who chooses to follow Him will be able to live with Him forever.

Teaching Tips

1. If you've ever tried to help a bird or animal, share the story. It will help the children understand that Jesus chose to become something less than what He was in order to save the people He created.

2. Try to explain Jesus' life of sinlessness at a level children can understand. He didn't become angry when people teased Him. He was always kind to those around Him. Whenever He saw someone in need, He helped. Ask, What would Jesus be like if He went to your school or lived in your house?

3. Read for yourself or, if appropriate, read aloud to the children selections from chapters 7 and 9 in *The Desire of Ages* or in *Messiah* to learn more about what Jesus' life was like when He was a child.

4. Share your favorite story from the life of Jesus.

Summary

Even though Jesus is still God, He became human so He could come to earth and save us. He lived like we do, but He never sinned. Then He died to pay for our sins.

The Holy Spirit

Bible Verse

"The wind blows where it wants to and you hear the sound of it, but you don't know where the wind comes from or where it is going. It is the same with every person who is born from the [Holy] Spirit."

— John 3:8

Have you ever been in a snowstorm? One winter at my house, we had a storm that was so strong that we had thunder and lightning and snow all at the same time! The wind was blowing very hard, and it was snowing so much that the wind was solid white. I almost got lost in my own front yard! But I wasn't really seeing the wind that night, just the snow.

You can see the leaves of a tree moving when the wind blows, and you can see the wind push clouds of dust or fog. But you can't really see the wind. All you can see is what it does.

The Holy Spirit is like that. You can't see Him touching people, but you can see how people change when He touches them.

Like Jesus and God the Father, the Holy Spirit has always existed. He was there when the world was created. And He was there when Jesus was baptized. In fact, the Holy Spirit worked with people from the beginning.

It was the Holy Spirit who helped the people who wrote the books of the Bible. He helped them remember stories and understand God's messages. He helped them see God's plans for the future and share their thoughts and feelings in songs and poems.

The Holy Spirit works on people's hearts. He reminds us how much God loves us. He teaches us how to live like Jesus. We can't see the Holy Spirit working, but we can see what happens when people listen to Him in their thoughts. When someone who used to be angry and selfish becomes a kind person who shares with others, the Holy Spirit has been working on that person's heart.

Jesus promised His disciples that the Holy Spirit would come after He went back to heaven. He said, "But the Helper will teach you everything and will cause you to remember all that I told you. This Helper is the Holy Spirit whom the Father will send in my name" (John 14:26).

With the Holy Spirit's help, the disciples remembered all the things that Jesus said, and they taught everyone around them about Jesus. The Holy Spirit does that for us too. He helps us remember the things that Jesus said and did. He helps us become like Jesus.

Teaching Tips

1. Show how the wind moves objects by using soap bubbles either outdoors in the wind or indoors with a fan. Ask, Can you see the wind? No? Then how do we know it's there? The answer is that we see how the wind affects the bubbles. In the same way, even though we can't see the Holy Spirit, we can see His effects—we can see how He changes people. (If it's appropriate, give each child soap bubbles and have a contest to see whose bubble travels the farthest before it pops.)

2. Jesus called the Holy Spirit the "Comforter" and the "Helper." Why does the Holy Spirit have these names? When would He comfort someone? When would He help?

3. The Holy Spirit helps us remember the Bible stories about Jesus and the things Jesus said. He gives us courage when we want to tell other people about Jesus.

Summary

The Holy Spirit works to change our hearts and make us more like Jesus. He speaks in our mind, showing us the way to be like Jesus.

Creation

In the beginning God created the heavens and the earth.

— Genesis 1:1, NIV

God created everything. He created everything you can see in the sky—the moon, the stars, and the planets. And He created everything you can't see in the sky—the empty space between the stars and the gravity that spins the planets around the sun.

God created everything you can see on earth—the trees, the rocks, the penguins, and the butterflies. And He created everything you can't see on earth—the bottom of the ocean, the inside of a mountain, and the cells that make up our bodies.

When God decided to create humans, He started with a special seven-day week. Each day, He created another part of the world that the humans would live in. On the first day, He created light. On the second day, He put the sky between the ground and outer space. On the third day, He gathered all the water together into rivers and lakes and oceans and left the ground dry. And on the dry ground, He made plants of all kinds grow.

On the fourth day, God created daytime and nighttime by hanging the sun and moon in the sky. On the fifth day, He filled the water with fish and whales and dolphins, and He filled the air with birds of every size and color.

On the sixth day, God created animals. Some ran across the ground. Some dug holes in it. Some climbed the trees or hid in the bushes. Then, when everything else was done, God created humans. First He created Adam, and then He created Eve.

"This is your planet," God told them. "You and your children must take care of it."

The work of creating the world was all done, but God wasn't finished. He had one more thing to make. The Bible says, "In six days the Lord made everything—the sky, the earth, the sea, and everything in them. On the seventh day he rested. So the Lord blessed the Sabbath day and made it holy" (Exodus 20:11).

On the seventh day, God stopped working and rested. This day is called the Sabbath. It is a holy day—a time to stop doing what we do the other six days and to think about what God has done for us. It's a time to remember that He created us and the world we live in. It's a time to remember that when we needed help, Jesus came to save us.

Teaching Tips

1. This is a wonderful time to remind children of the beauty and variety in nature. A trip to the zoo or a walk in the woods would be a delightful way to enjoy God's creation.

2. Engage the children's creativity by having them draw an animal or bird they would have asked God to create.

3. Help the children make a list of things they enjoy doing on Sabbath that helps them remember what God has done for us.

Summary

God is the Creator of everything. In six days, He created the world and gave it to humans to care for. Then He created the Sabbath, a time to rest and remember Him.

What Humans Are Like

Bible Verse

God created human beings in his image. In the image of God he created them. He created them male and female.

— Genesis 1:27

Have you ever built a frog house? When I was a Primary, I built frog houses in the dirt under the sycamore tree in my backyard. Here's how you do it.

First, you need nice soft dirt that's a little bit wet. Not goopy mud, but wet enough so that the dirt sticks together. Scoop out a hole just big enough for your two feet to fit inside. Then pack the dirt you dug out back on top of your feet. Pat the dirt down nice and hard until it's smooth on top. Then slide your feet out very slowly. If you're careful, you'll have a nice quiet cave with a roof over the top—just right for a frog house!

I don't think any frogs ever moved into my frog houses, but I had fun making them. Of course, they weren't really houses. But they did have a roof and room inside like a house does, so they were like houses.

God did something like that when He created humans. The Bible says He created them in His image—like Him. "God created human beings in his image. In the image of God he created them. He created them male and female" (Genesis 1:27).

So humans were created to be like God. We don't know if that means God has two arms and legs like we do or if it means that God laughs and sings like we do. We do know that God made humans to live forever, to be happy and free.

We're free to choose whether we like green or blue better. We're free to choose whether we like dogs or cats more. All humans are also free to follow God and trust Him or to go their own way and trust themselves.

Adam and Eve chose not to trust God. They disobeyed God and sinned. Something inside them that was like God changed and became sinful. God could forgive them, but He couldn't stop the results of their choice. By choosing sin, they chose the sadness and pain and death that come with it. All humans born since then are sinful, including you and me.

But Jesus came to save us from sin! By following Him, we can become more like God again, like Adam and Eve were in the beginning. When we follow Jesus, we love God, we are kind to each other, and we take care of the world around us—even the frogs!

Teaching Tips

1. If you have a nice patch of clean dirt or a sandbox, try making frog houses with the children. It's fun!

2. Have the children make a list of their favorite color, animal, bird, fruit, and kind of weather. Remind them that we are all free to choose what we like, and we are free to choose whether to follow God.

3. Children this age find the concept of being sinful difficult to understand. You might focus instead on the effects of sin—pain, sickness, and death—and how Jesus came to save us from all those things.

Summary

God created us to be like Him. Because Adam and Eve sinned, though, all humans became sinful, and pain and sickness and death came to everyone. But Jesus came to save us from sin and put an end to those things.

The War Between Jesus and Satan

Bible Verse

There was a war in heaven. . . . The giant dragon [Satan] was thrown down out of heaven.

— Revelation 12:7, 9

Have you ever had a fight with your brother or sister or with a friend? Well, the fight between Jesus and Satan is not like that at all. In this battle, Jesus is fighting to show that God is fair and kind, while Satan is fighting to make people believe God is unfair and mean.

God created the universe with love. And He gave people and angels freedom to choose. People can choose to love each other and to love God—or they can choose to be mean to each other and to hate God. Lucifer, the most important angel in heaven, was the first to choose not to believe God. Lucifer liked being important and telling everyone what to do. But he didn't like anyone telling him what to do. Not even God. "I'm smart enough to do what I want," he told the other angels. "And if we're really free like God says, He has to let me do what I want."

God talked to Lucifer. "I love you," He said, "and you are free to choose. But if you choose hate instead of love, you'll die."

Lucifer wouldn't listen. And many of the angels agreed with him. Lucifer and his angels broke God's laws of love. So God couldn't let them live in heaven anymore. The Bible says, "There was a war in heaven" (Revelation 12:7). Jesus threw Lucifer and his angels out. From then on, Lucifer was known as Satan.

Satan watched as Jesus created Adam and Eve. He listened when Jesus told them,

"You can eat fruit from any tree in the garden except this one. If you eat this fruit, you will die." The fruit wasn't poison. It was a test. Would Adam and Eve trust God or listen to Satan?

Of course, you know that Eve ate the fruit. So did Adam.

"See," Satan said to God, "no one can keep Your laws. Either You have to kill everyone or You have to let everyone do whatever they want—even sin—forever."

But Jesus and His Father had made a plan. Jesus would come to earth as a baby and grow up just like any other person. He would teach everyone that they could trust God, that they would be happy if they obeyed His laws of love.

Then, even though He was perfect, Jesus would die so humans didn't have to. Anyone who believes in Him and trusts Him can live forever just like God planned. Jesus fought the war with Satan by becoming a human and keeping God's laws of love. He proved God is fair and right. By dying for humans, He showed how much God really loves them.

Teaching Tips

1. It's important that children understand that the war between Jesus and Satan is not like a physical battle. Review what they are fighting to show (Jesus is fighting to show that God is fair and kind, while Satan is fighting to make people believe that God is unfair and mean) and how Jesus fought (by becoming human and keeping God's laws of love).

2. Have the children draw a picture of Satan as a snake in the tree and Eve looking at the fruit. Then have them write on the picture what they wish Eve had said to the snake.

Summary

When Lucifer chose not to follow God anymore, he and his angels were thrown out of heaven. As Satan, he tempted Adam and Eve to doubt God, and they sinned too. But Jesus fought back by becoming a human, living a perfect life, and then dying to pay for our sins.

Jesus Lived, Died, and Lives Again

"God loved the world so much that he gave his one and only Son so that whoever believes in him may not be lost, but have eternal life."

— John 3:16

Adam chose to listen to Satan instead of Jesus. And because of that, the whole world became sinful. Animals began to fight with each other. Thorns started growing on plants. Things started to die. People started to get old and sick and die.

So God stepped in with His plan. The Bible says, "God loved the world so much that he gave his one and only Son so that whoever believes in him may not be lost, but have eternal life" (John 3:16).

God gave Jesus to us. Jesus was born on earth like any human baby. He grew up like all the other kids in His town. But He wasn't just like them. He was human, like you and me, but He was still God, too.

Jesus taught people that they could trust God because God loves them very much. And He lived His whole life on earth without sinning. He never did anything wrong. He always followed God's plans for His life. By living that way, He showed us that we don't have to be God's enemies. We can follow God every day just like He did.

Because Adam and Eve sinned, all humans born on earth became God's enemies. They would all grow old and die. And even worse, they would die forever and never get to live in heaven.

Jesus never sinned. He wasn't God's enemy. But because He loved all humans very much, He said, "I'll die so you don't have to. I'll take your punishment for sinning. You can take my reward for following God and live in heaven forever."

So Jesus let bad people arrest Him and beat Him and nail Him to a cross made of wood. He died there so that we can live forever in heaven if we want to. All we have to do is ask Him to save us and give ourselves to Him.

Jesus died and He was buried. But He didn't stay dead. On the third day after He died, Jesus came back to life. He proved that God is stronger than Satan. He proved that everyone who belongs to Him will live forever in heaven, no matter what happens to them on earth.

Jesus lived for us—He showed us how to follow God. Jesus died for us—He took our punishment and gave us His reward. Jesus came to life again—He proved God is stronger than Satan and that heaven is a promise He can keep.

Teaching Tips

1. If possible, provide a small box and wrapping paper for each child. Say, God loved us so much that He gave us His Son Jesus. If you could give God a gift, what would it be? Have them write their answer on a slip of paper, place the paper inside the box, and wrap their gift for God.

2. Ask the children these questions: What would it be like to have Jesus as a friend in your class at school or in your Sabbath School class? What would He do at recess? What would He do at lunchtime?

3. Alternate activity: Read the story of the resurrection from a child-friendly Bible. Then ask the children to draw a picture of the morning Jesus came back to life. Remind them to include the angels and the stone rolled away and the Roman soldiers who were guarding Jesus' grave.

Summary

Before God and Jesus created this world and its people, They made a "just-in-case" plan. They planned how they would rescue people if the people chose to follow Satan and become sinners—enemies of God.

How God Saves People

The Father has loved us so much that we are called children of God. And we really are his children.

— 1 John 3:1

Do you know what it means to be adopted? My family had a dog named Jazz that adopted a kitten named Tiger. When we brought little Tiger home from the animal shelter, Jazz didn't like her. Jazz barked once and then walked away.

Little Tiger didn't like to be alone, so when we weren't holding her, she would cry. When Jazz heard her meowing, she came to see what the fuss was all about.

Tiger liked Jazz, and she would try to follow the dog everywhere it went. At first, Jazz didn't care what Tiger did. She would run off barking or playing and leave the kitten behind. But every time Jazz lay down to rest, Tiger was there, purring and snuggling in beside her.

Before long, Jazz was treating Tiger like her own puppy. They would play together, eat together, and sleep in the same spot. Jazz adopted the kitten into her family—even though kittens didn't really belong there—and they were friends for years.

God does the same thing for us when He offers to give us salvation. Salvation is a big word that means "being saved" or "being rescued." Just as you can rescue people from drowning by pulling them out of the water, God rescues us from sin by adopting us into His family.

All of us are sinners. We are born to be enemies of God. But God loves us anyway. The Bible says, "God shows his great love for us in this way: Christ died for us while we were still sinners" (Romans 5:8).

Even while we were God's enemies and didn't belong in His family, God wanted us there. He adopts us into His family when we say, "I love Jesus, and I believe He died to rescue me from sin." Then we ask God to forgive us for the things we've done that are bad or mean, and we ask Him to change us so we'll always be like Jesus.

That makes us part of God's family! And when we're part of God's family, we can plan on going to heaven and living with Him forever.

God has a special plan to help us live like Jesus did. He sent the Holy Spirit to teach us. The Holy Spirit speaks in our hearts, helping us learn about Jesus and helping us remember to live like Jesus did, always being kind to others and always trusting in God.

Teaching Tips

1. Share a story you have about unusual animal friends or ask the children for stories they may know. Remind them how God accepts us into His family.

2. Ask, Can you remember a time when you were in danger and someone rescued you? or share a rescue story of your own. Then review with the children what salvation or being saved means.

3. Show the children how to create a family tree. Then tell them to make the tree with many branches because they can place on it anyone they'd like to have in their family. Remind them to include relatives, friends, church members, and God.

Summary

Even when we were His enemies, God loved us and sent Jesus to save us. When we accept Jesus, He adopts us into His family.

Growing in Jesus

We all show the Lord's glory, and we are being changed to be like him.

— 2 Corinthians 3:18

Have you ever planted a seed and watched it grow? Once I planted a bean in the flowerbed outside my window. (I didn't tell my mom!) I watered it and watched it, and after a few days in the warm sun, it sprouted and began to grow. Every day it grew more leaves and became taller.

But one morning when I looked out my window, my plant was dead! I ran outside to see what had happened and found my enemy. It was a big green caterpillar. It had chewed my little plant right off at the ground.

Seeds sprout and grow when they have dirt and water and sunshine. But they still need protection from their enemies—insects who like to eat them for lunch.

Christians are like those seeds. We can grow to be more like Jesus, but we need protection from our enemy—Satan. And Jesus works better than the best bug spray in the world!

While Jesus lived on earth, He had to fight with Satan and his evil demons many times. It was never a punching or kicking kind of fight—there was no need for that. When Jesus told Satan to leave, Satan ran away. But he kept trying to hurt Jesus.

Satan tried to trick Jesus in the desert. He and the other evil angels controlled the minds of some people and made them hurt themselves and others. But when Jesus saw these people, He commanded the evil angels to leave, and they did.

When Jesus died on the cross, Satan thought that he had won. But he hadn't. By dying for the people that He loved, Jesus won the battle over evil. He won, and that means someday Satan and all his evil forces will be destroyed forever.

Because Jesus has already won this fight, we are winners too. When we follow Him and live with the Holy Spirit in our hearts, we have the power to push the evil forces away whenever they tempt us to do wrong. We don't have to be afraid of what Satan can do because Jesus has already beaten him.

Every day we can grow to be more like Jesus. We grow when we talk to Him in prayer, when we study the Bible, when we sing songs to praise Him, and when we worship together in church. When we help people around us and tell them about God's love, Jesus is with us every minute of every day.

Teaching Tips

1. If possible, help the children plant bean seeds in plastic cups. As the seeds sprout and grow, use them to remind the children how we grow to be more like Jesus.

2. Ask, What enemies do plants have? (insects, lack of water, animals that eat plants, lack of nutrients/fertilizer, and more) Then ask, What enemy do we, as Christians, have, and why we don't need to be afraid of this enemy?

3. Have the children draw a line down the middle of a sheet of paper. On one side, list the things that make plants grow. On the other side, list what makes us grow to be more like Jesus.

Summary

Because Jesus defeated Satan on the cross, we can defeat him also. By depending on the Holy Spirit, we can grow to be more like Jesus every day.

God's Family on Earth

Bible Verse

You should not stay away from the church meetings . . . but you should meet together and encourage each other.

— Hebrews 10:25

How big is your family? I have two brothers and two sisters, so I always thought I had a big family—especially when I had to wait for my turn for something! But then one summer, my father's sister came to visit. Her three children—my cousins—were also part of my family. In fact, my father had three sisters, and all their children made my family bigger than I had imagined.

But guess what? My mother had seven brothers and sisters! When all of them—all my aunts and uncles and cousins—got together, there were more people than I could count.

Our church is like a family. It's God's family on earth. But this family is bigger than just the people you go to Sabbath School with. It's bigger than all the families that sit in the all the pews or chairs in your church. God's family on earth includes all the people in all the Adventist churches in the world. Millions of Adventists go to church every week, and they are all part of your family.

But our family is even bigger than that! God's family on earth includes people from many different churches. It includes people who live in big cities and people who live in forests. It includes people who shovel snow every winter and people who have to put on sunscreen lotion every day. It includes people with white hair and people with black hair, people with blue eyes and people with brown eyes, people with dark skin and people with light skin.

It includes everyone in the world who loves Jesus, everyone who is learning to follow Him!

We meet together in church to praise God, to learn from the Bible, and to enjoy spending time with the other people in our big family. We may have pastors or other church leaders, but the Person who is the real Leader of our church is Jesus.

The Bible says that the church is like a person's body, and Jesus is the head. "Speaking the truth with love, we will grow up in every way into Christ, who is the head. The whole body depends on Christ, and all the parts of the body are joined and held together" (Ephesians 4:15, 16).

Best of all, the Bible promises that Jesus is returning to earth soon to take His family to heaven to live with Him forever.

Teaching Tips

1. Have all the children count how many people are in their families. They can start with their own home, and then add grandparents, cousins, aunts, uncles, etc. Don't hesitate to allow children to count stepfamilies as they wish.

2. Using a map or globe, help the children get an idea of how big their Adventist family is. Find out how many members there are in your church, in your conference, and in your union. There are more than one million members in North America, and more than fourteen million worldwide. To get up-to-date information about Adventists in each country in the world, go to www.adventist.org.

3. Ask the children to list the different kinds of people in their local church family. Prompt them to notice that the family is made up of young and old people, tall and short people, people of different nationalities, skin colors, etc. Use this to point out that while our own families may look and act alike, God's family is made up of many different kinds of people.

Summary

Everyone who loves Jesus and is learning to follow Him is a part of God's family on earth. This family is made up of many different kinds of people, and Jesus is our Leader.

The Last Ones Left

Bible Verse

God's holy people must be patient. They must obey God's commands and keep their faith in Jesus.

— Revelation 14:12

Have you ever played kick-the-can? It's a little like hide-and-seek and a little like capture-the-flag. One person closes their eyes and counts while everyone else runs to hide. The person who is "it" has to try to find everyone without letting anyone kick the can. If the person who is "it" sees you, you have to race to kick the can before they can reach it again. If they get to the can first, you're out of the game. But if you kick it before they can get there, you win!

One day we were playing kick-the-can, and my brother was "it." He was fast—too fast for most of the rest of us to outrun, so everyone was being caught. Finally, my cousin Hoss and I were the only ones left.

"Let's try something," I whispered to him. "You go around the house on this side, and I'll go around the other side. We'll both stick our hands around the corners and wave. If he runs toward you, I'll come behind him and kick the can. If he runs toward me, you do it."

So we each snuck to our corners and waved. When my brother ran toward Hoss's side of the house, I raced as fast as I could and kicked the can. I was the last one left, so I won!

Jesus promised to come back to earth to take His people to heaven. But He also said that earth would become a very bad place just before He came back. During the end time—the time just before Jesus comes—most people will forget about God and do whatever they want, even if it's evil and selfish.

The last people left who still love Jesus, who still keep His commandments and follow Him faithfully, will have a special job. They will have to tell the world that Jesus is coming back. They will warn the others in the world that the day of the Lord—the day Jesus returns—is coming.

This will be their warning: "The day of the Lord will come like a thief. The skies will disappear with a loud noise. Everything in them will be destroyed by fire, and the earth and everything in it will be burned up" (2 Peter 3:10).

The last ones left—the remnant—will do more than just warn people. They will keep telling everyone how much Jesus loves them. And no matter what bad things happen, they will faithfully follow Jesus. Would you like to be one of the remnant—one of the last people left to tell the world that Jesus is coming? You can be if you just keep following Him every day!

Teaching Tips

1. If it's appropriate, play a game with the children in which the winner is the last one left (e.g., musical chairs or hide-and-seek). Afterward, remind them that the last ones left who are followers of Jesus will have a special job at the end of time. Discuss how they can continue to study and learn about Jesus and tell others about Him.

2. Help the children make a newspaper that reports the stories of the last days. Assign a child or a group of children to write about bad things happening, such as wars and disasters, and people doing selfish and evil things, and about the people who are still telling others about Jesus and His love for them. You may also want to have the children draw pictures to go with their stories. Paste the stories and pictures onto a big sheet to make the front page of a newspaper.

Summary

The remnant—the last ones left on earth who love and follow Jesus—will have a special work to do in the last days.

Together in the Family

Bible Verse

We are many, but in Christ we are all one body.

— Romans 12:5

You have two eyes and two ears. You have ten fingers and ten toes. You have a heart that pumps blood through your body and lungs to breathe the air. Do you know how many bones you have in your body? When the human body is finished growing, it has 206 bones.

With all your teeth and all your hair and all your skin, your body has many, many different parts. And all those parts have to work together to keep you strong and healthy.

It would be silly for your ears to say, "Hey, we're tired of being on the side of the head. We want to be in front and see things like the eyes do." Or for your toes to say, "We're tired of just kicking things. We want to catch and throw things like the fingers do."

Our bodies don't work that way. Each of our parts is different, and each one is important to making the whole body work right.

The church is like that also. It's like a body, and all the people who belong to it are its parts. Just like the parts of our body are different, people in the church are different also. They come from many different countries and speak many languages. Some are tall and some are short. Some have curly hair and some have straight hair. Some have darker skin and some have lighter skin.

They come from different families, but when they join God's church, they all become members of one big family. In the church, it doesn't matter if you are a boy or a girl, if you're rich or poor, or if you like broccoli or bananas better! All that matters is that you're part of the family.

The Bible says, "Each one of us has a body with many parts, and these parts all have different uses. In the same way, we are many, but in Christ we are all one body. Each one is a part of that body, and each part belongs to all the other parts" (Romans 12: 4, 5).

Because we all love God, we share the same faith—that Jesus came to save us. We share the same hope—that Jesus is coming back someday soon to take us all to heaven. And because of this, we all share the same job—we want to tell everyone else in the world about Jesus.

Because God the Father, Jesus, and the Holy Spirit are working together to save humans, we want to work together to help Them. No matter who we are, we work together as a church to invite everyone else to come and join God's family.

Summary

The church is made of many different people, but they all work together to tell the world about Jesus.

Teaching Tips

1. Have the children draw what faces would look like if the features were mixed up—if the ears wanted to be eyes and the eyes wanted to be teeth, for example. Along with the fun, point out that each part of the body has to do its job if everything is going to work.

2. If possible, have the children interview several church members to find out more about them. Have them ask questions like What's your favorite food? How old were you when you were baptized? How many people are in your family? What do you like most about church?

3. Ask, How do church members work together, and what things do they do together to tell the world about Jesus?

Baptism

Bible Verse

"Repent and be baptized, every one of you, in the name of Jesus Christ for the forgiveness of your sins. And you will receive the gift of the Holy Spirit."

— Acts 2:38, NIV

Do you like to eat sunflower seeds? I do. I like to eat the ones that are still inside their shells. They're so small that I can put one right between my teeth and bite down. Crack! The shell splits in half, and out comes the seed. Yummy!

One summer I wanted to grow a sunflower plant and pick the seeds for myself. So I buried the seeds down under the dirt by the fence, watered the ground, and waited. Soon the tiny green plants were reaching up into the sky. I kept them watered, and every day they grew a little more.

When I planted my seeds, I thought the sunflower was a short little plant with a big flower. Was I ever wrong! My sunflower plants kept growing until they were taller than me—even taller than the fence. And the flowers that bloomed at the top of the plants weren't just big. They were bigger around than the biggest plates in our kitchen!

Baptism is a little like planting a sunflower seed. If we want to grow and become kind and beautiful people like Jesus is, we have to be planted or buried like the seed was. But when we're baptized, we're not buried in dirt. We're buried in water.

We believe in being baptized like Jesus was—we go down under the water and come back up. When we go under the water, the person we used to be dies. When we come up out of the water, it's like coming back to life. And like the sunflower seed when it sprouts, we're different. All the things we've done wrong—our sins—

are forgiven. Now we're ready to grow and become more like Jesus every day.

When we choose to be baptized, we're telling everyone that we believe Jesus died for us and came back to life and is planning to take us to heaven some day.

When you're baptized, you're telling everyone that you have studied what the Bible teaches and you believe it. That's why most of us go to baptismal classes first, so we really do know what the Bible teaches.

One of the things the Bible teaches is that we should be baptized. When people wanted to be followers of Jesus, Peter told them, "Repent and be baptized, every one of you, in the name of Jesus Christ for the forgiveness of your sins. And you will receive the gift of the Holy Spirit" (Acts 2:38, NIV).

That's a gift you will get too when you are baptized. The Holy Spirit will help you understand the Bible. It will help you obey your parents. It will help you grow just like my sunflower did—taller and taller, more and more beautiful, more and more like Jesus every day.

Summary

The Bible teaches that we should be baptized to show the world that we choose Jesus as our Savior and that we want to grow to be more like Him.

Teaching Tips

1. If possible, show the children a sunflower with the seeds still inside so they can learn how the seeds grow. If not, share some sunflower seeds (or other seeds), and encourage the children to plant them at home.

2. The idea that baptism is like being buried and being brought back to life may be confusing. Use the idea of being buried like a seed and sprouting up like a new plant to help the children understand what baptism means.

3. Have the children draw flowers with their faces and the faces of their friends and family in the center of the blossoms. At the top of the page, have them write, I'm growing to be more like Jesus.

4. This would be a good time to ask if any of the children are interested in studying to be baptized.

Jesus' Last Supper

Bible Verse

Every time you eat this bread and drink this cup you are telling others about the Lord's death until he comes.

— 1 Corinthians 11:26

On the last night before Jesus died, He had a special supper with His disciples. Because it was special, everyone dressed in their best robe. But in those days, people wore sandals—so their feet were dirty when they sat down to eat. Most of the time, at special meals, someone hired a servant to wash the feet of the people before they ate. But on this night, there were no servants.

The disciples hadn't listened when Jesus told them that He was going to die. They wanted Him to make Himself king of their country. They sat and argued about who was going to have the most important job in Jesus' kingdom.

Jesus had to make them stop thinking about themselves and listen to Him. He stood up and wrapped a towel around His waist. Then He picked up a big bowl of water and started washing the disciples' feet. They stopped talking and stared. They wanted Jesus to be their king—but He was acting like their servant!

When Jesus was finished, they sat quietly and listened to Him. "Do you understand what I did tonight?" He asked. "The greatest people in my kingdom are the ones who serve each other, the ones who take care of each other."

Then Jesus picked up a loaf of bread and started tearing off pieces for them. "This bread is like My body, which I am giving up for you. When you eat it, think about what I've done for you." Next, Jesus picked up a cup of grape juice. "This juice is like my blood, which I will bleed for you. When you drink it, remember Me."

Ever since that night, Christians have repeated this special meal to remember what Jesus said and what He did for us when He died on the cross. We repeat the foot washing that Jesus did with His disciples. It reminds us that we should take care of each other and love each other the way Jesus loves each one of us. And when we share the bread and juice, we remember that Jesus promised to come back soon. The Bible says, "Every time you eat this bread and drink this cup you are telling others about the Lord's death until he comes" (1 Corinthians 11:26).

Teaching Tips

1. Set up a Communion service for the children. If possible, invite the pastor to tell the story of Jesus and the Last Supper to them as he explains what the service means.

2. Ask, What did Jesus mean when He said that the greatest people in God's kingdom are the ones who take care of others? Who are the greatest people in the church? Who are the greatest people in your family?

3. Create an appropriate service project for the children. Suggestions: They might pick up trash in the church parking lot, help at the church's community service center, pick up the offering for a church service, or help serve and clean up after a potluck. Remind the children that those who serve others are the greatest in God's kingdom.

Summary

We share the Lord's Supper to remember what Jesus said and what He did for us on the cross. Foot washing reminds us to care for each other the way Jesus did.

Special Gifts to Work for God

Each of you has received a gift to use to serve others.

— 1 Peter 4:10

Isn't it fun to see a gift all wrapped in bright paper with your name on it? Have you ever tried to guess what was inside your present before you opened it?

Once I accidentally found a present with my name on it the week before my birthday. The box wasn't very big, but it was heavy. I shook it, and it rattled a little. So I shook it harder. It rattled some more. But I still couldn't tell what it was. So, I shook it really hard—and this time I heard a lot of rattling! In fact, it sounded like it broke into a hundred pieces! I quickly pushed it back under the bed and left it alone.

When my birthday came, I opened my other presents first. That was fun, but I kept worrying about that last gift. What was it? And was it broken to bits? Finally, I tore the paper off and carefully opened the box. It was a flashlight! Well, it was the parts of a flashlight. But it wasn't broken. I put the batteries in and screwed the top on, and it worked just fine.

I really liked that flashlight because I knew what it meant. Now when it was time for someone to go out to the barn to check on the cows or to the shed to check on the chickens after dark, I would get to go. Because I got that gift, I knew I had an important job to do.

Earlier in this book, we talked about how a body needs eyes and ears and hands and feet if it's going to work right. We learned that God's church is like that—it needs many different kinds of people if it's going to work right.

God gives all the people in His church special talents—special things they can do. The Bible calls them gifts. They're like presents from God that you don't get to open right away. Some you might open while you grow up, some not until later. There are many jobs that must be done if the church is going to do the work Jesus gave us to do. When all the people in the church use their special gifts together, then everyone has fun and they do Jesus' work.

The Bible says, "We all have different gifts. . . . The person who has the gift of prophecy should use that gift in agreement with the faith. Anyone who has the gift of serving should serve. Anyone who has the gift of teaching should teach. Whoever has the gift of encouraging others should encourage. Whoever has the gift of giving to others should give freely. Anyone who has the gift of being a leader should try hard when he leads. Whoever has the gift of showing mercy to others should do so with joy" (Romans 12:6–8).

You may not know what gifts God has given you, but He already has them wrapped up with your name on them. When you see what special gift you have, then you'll know what work God wants you to do.

Teaching Tips

1. Ask each child, Tell us about a gift you've gotten that you really liked. Remind them that God has a gift for each of them, a talent they will discover when they become older.

2. Help children match the following gifts with people at church or people they know: gift of helping others, gift of teaching, gift of kindness, gift of being a leader, gift of giving.

3. Have the children make Thank-you cards for people in the church who use their gifts for God. Suggest cards for the pastor, Sabbath School teacher, church janitor, potluck coordinator, VBS leader, church organist or pianist, etc.

Summary

God gives each one of us special gifts or talents so that we can work for Him.

A Messenger for God

Bible Verse

Do not hold back the work of the Holy Spirit. Do not treat prophecy as if it were unimportant.

— 1 Thessalonians 5:19, 20

In the last chapter, we talked about the gifts God gives us, the special talents He gives us so we can do work for Him and help others. One of those special gifts is the gift of prophecy—that is, to be a prophet for God.

What do prophets do? In the Bible, some prophets, like Daniel, told about things that would happen in the future. Other prophets, like Samuel or Elisha, were leaders and teachers, telling everyone how God wants them to live. Some prophets, like John and Peter, did both. Sometimes God sent the prophets dreams while they were sleeping; sometimes they saw visions (like a dream, except you're not asleep); and sometimes they heard God's voice.

Since the days of the Bible, God has not given many people the gift of being a prophet. But the Bible says that He will.

> *In the last days, God says,*
> *I will pour out my Spirit on all people.*
> *Your sons and daughters will prophesy,*
> *your young men will see visions,*
> *your old men will dream dreams.*
> *Even on my servants, both men and women,*
> *I will pour out my Spirit in those days,*
> *and they will prophesy.* — Acts 2:17, 18, NIV

Our church started because people believed that the end of the world was near and that Jesus was coming soon. We still believe that we're living in the last days and years before Jesus comes. And since Jesus is coming soon, it isn't surprising that God gave someone the job of being a prophet. God gave the gift of prophecy to a young woman named Ellen. With the man she married, James White, and an old sea captain named Joseph Bates, she helped our church get started.

Ellen White had visions and dreams. She wrote down the things she saw and heard, and she shared what she wrote with all the new Adventist people. But most of her work was teaching people, helping them understand the Bible and understand how to live like Jesus.

Even though Ellen White died long ago, we still have her books and writings today, and they still help us understand how to follow God faithfully. She taught us to put the Bible first and to obey its teachings. When God gave her the gift of prophecy, He gave her messages that have helped our church grow around the world.

Teaching Tips

1. Ask the children, If God gave you a message to share with other people, what do you think that message would be? Do you think people would listen to you and believe you? Why or why not?

2. Have the children draw pictures that answer this question: If you were trying to share a message from God with people around the world, how would you send that message? (Answers would include television, radio, Internet, singing, preaching, talking, etc.)

3. Find a way for the children to share God's message of love with someone. You might take them to visit a shut-in member or a nursing home or have the children make cards about God's love.

4. Share a story from the book *Ellen* by Mabel Miller, one of Paul Ricchiuti's books about Ellen White, or another book about her.

Summary

God gave Ellen White the gift of prophecy. He gave her messages that have helped our church grow around the world.

God's Laws

Loving God means obeying his commands. And God's commands are not too hard for us.

— 1 John 5:3

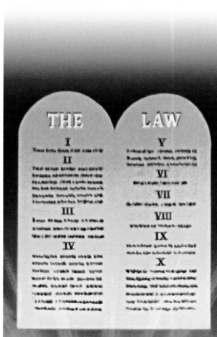

I broke the law last month. I was driving too fast on the freeway. A police car followed me with its red and blue lights flashing, and I had to pull over to the side of the road. The police officer walked up to my window. "Did you know you were speeding?" he asked.

"Yes, Officer," I had to say. He wrote me a ticket and told me to slow down. I did drive slower after that, but I still had to pay a lot of money because of the ticket.

Why did the police officer give me a ticket? Because he was mean? Because he didn't like me? No. He did it to protect me. He knew that everyone driving on the road, including me, would be safer if I would drive slower.

When God created this world, He made it with laws: The sun comes up every day. Rain falls down from the sky. These are some of the laws that keep our planet alive.

God created laws for people too. He didn't make the laws to be mean or just to tell people what to do. He made laws that would keep people happy and healthy.

We find God's laws in the Bible. In Exodus 20, God gave us the Ten Commandments—ten rules to live by. When someone asked Jesus which of the rules was most important, He said, " 'Love the Lord your God with all your heart, all your soul, and all your mind.' This is the first and most important command. And the second command is like the first: 'Love your neighbor as you love yourself'" (Matthew 22:37–39).

Jesus showed us that keeping God's laws means doing what God wants us to do. Instead of being angry at others, we can be nice no matter how they act. That's what Jesus did. Instead of being selfish, we can share with others. That's what Jesus did. When we have a chance to help someone or be friendly, we can be kind. That's what Jesus did.

The people who go to heaven some day will be the ones who wanted more than anything to be like Jesus. When we are following Jesus, we are obeying God's laws.

Teaching Tips

1. Share a story about some time when you got in trouble for breaking the law or breaking a rule and tell what you learned. Emphasize the purpose of the law or rule that was broken and that it was meant to protect you or others.

2. Ask the children, What are some of the rules at your house (or school)? Do these rules protect you? If you could make the rules, what rules would you make?

3. Collect a variety of common objects around the house, such as scissors, a kitchen knife, a bottle of pills, a bottle of kitchen cleaner, a ball, a Bible, keys, etc., and place them in a bag. One by one, have each child pull an item from the bag and then come up with a rule about it.

Summary

God's laws protect our health and happiness. When we are following Jesus, we are obeying God's laws.

Sabbath: Earth's Birthday Party

Bible Verse

"You should call the Sabbath a joyful day and honor it as the Lord's holy day. . . . Then you will find joy in the Lord."

— Isaiah 58:13, 14

When is your birthday? Mine is in October, and every year, I have a party to celebrate. Sometimes I get presents!

Don't you like birthday parties? When it's your birthday, you might get presents or have a cake or ice cream or maybe some of your favorite food. But the most fun part of a birthday party is having your friends and family come and be with you.

You have a birthday once a year to celebrate the day you were born. How would you like to have a birthday every week?

When God created the world, He spent six days making monkeys and oceans and trees and flowers and lions and sheep and butterflies and turtles and everything else. "By the seventh day, God finished the work he had been doing, so he rested from all his work. God blessed the seventh day and made it a holy day, because on that day he rested from all the work he had done in creating the world" (Genesis 2:2, 3).

On your birthday, your family and friends celebrate how happy they are that you were born. On the seventh day of the week, Saturday, we celebrate how happy we are that God created the world and all the things in it (especially puppies and kittens!). We call the seventh day Sabbath.

But the Sabbath is more than just a party. It's a time to worship God and learn more about Him. It's a time to get together at church to sing and pray. It's a time to remember that Jesus wants to save us and take us home to live with Him in heaven.

Because the Sabbath is such a special day, we don't do the same things on Sabbath that we do on other days. The Bible says, "Remember to keep the Sabbath holy. Work and get everything done during six days each week, but the seventh day is a day of rest to honor the Lord your God" (Exodus 20:8–10).

The Sabbath is a special gift from God. When we remember Him on that day, He gives us a special blessing. Isn't that nice? On the earth's birthday, we get a present!

Teaching Tips

1. Ask, What are your favorite things to do on your birthday? What are your favorite things to do on the Sabbath, the earth's birthday?

2. Ask, What if on the day of your birthday, your parents said, "Happy birthday, but we're going to be busy cleaning the garage all day." How would you feel? How do you think God feels when we treat the Sabbath like any other day?

3. If possible, have a birthday party on Sabbath to celebrate Creation. Serve cake and give each child a flower to wear to church or a balloon to take home. Remind them to say to everyone they meet, "Happy birthday! It's Sabbath!"

Summary

The seventh-day Sabbath is a celebration of Creation. It's a holy day, when we set aside the things we normally do and take time to be with God.

Taking Care of God's Things

God loves the person who gives happily. And God can give you more blessings than you need.

— 2 Corinthians 9:7, 8

Have you ever made a toad trap? You take a big spoon and dig a hole in soft dirt. You make the sides of the hole really steep. That way, when a toad hops by and falls in, it can't jump out.

One summer, I dug a toad trap, and the next morning when I checked, two toads were in it! I fixed a nice wire cage for my new pets, with some grass and dirt for them to lie on. I played with them for a while, but since toads don't do much, I got bored. Then I wandered off and forgot all about them.

The next day, my mother called me over to their cage. "Look," she said. My toads were skinny and dry. They looked sick. "They haven't had any food or water," Mom said. "Why don't you let them go back in the flowerbed?"

I put the toads down in some nice mud next to the flowers, but I felt bad. The toads were my pets, and I hadn't taken care of them.

Whether you have a dog, a cat, a bird, or a lizard, a pet is something you have to take care of. You have to make sure they have food and water and a good place to sleep.

When God created Adam and Eve, He said, "This whole world filled with animals and plants is Mine. But I want you to take care of it for Me."

God says the same thing to us. He gave us animals and trees to enjoy. He gives us bodies and brains. He gives us talents so we can sing and speak and draw pictures and run and jump. He says, "I gave these things to you, and I want you to take care of them for Me."

To help us remember that He gave us everything, God asks us to give a little part back to Him. We call this tithe and offerings.

In Old Testament times, God said, "Bring to the storehouse a tenth of what you earn so there will be food in my house. ... I will open the windows of heaven for you and pour out all the blessings you need" (Malachi 3:10).

Today, God asks that we bring back to Him one tenth of what we earn using the talents He has given us. If we make one dollar, we give ten cents back to God. If we make ten dollars, we give one dollar back to God. This is called tithe. God promises that when we give our tithe faithfully, He'll give us more blessings than we have room to hold!

We can also give an offering from our money. This is a way to thank God for His blessings and to help pay for the work of telling others about Jesus. Offerings can be a little or a lot, but they always help us remember that God said, "Take care of things for Me."

Teaching Tips

1. Ask each child to share what kind of pet they have and how they care for that pet.

2. Ask, What talents do you think God has given you? How will you use those talents for God?

3. Give each child a sack of items—jelly beans, marbles, rocks. Then have them figure out how much is one tenth of whatever they have. For young children, you may need to keep the items in multiples of ten.

Summary

God gave us this earth, our bodies, and our talents. He wants us to care for them and use them to do His work. When we return tithes and give offerings, He blesses us.

Just Like Jesus

Whoever says that he lives in God must live as Jesus lived.

— 1 John 2:6

Let's play a game! Can you guess what kind of pet I have? My pet likes to play. Sometimes she races around the room as if she's chasing something I can't see. She likes to take a nap in the bright sunshine by the window. She eats and drinks from bowls on the kitchen floor. When she wants to go outside, she scratches on the door. Can you guess what kind of pet I have?

She doesn't chase cars or dig holes under the fence. When I throw a stick, she won't chase it and bring it back to me. She has a scratching post, and sometimes she likes to sit on top of the refrigerator.

Did you guess? At first, I could have been describing either a dog or a cat. But dogs do like to chase sticks, and they never climb on top of the refrigerator!

You could tell my pet is a cat by the way she behaved—by the things she did or didn't do. Being a Christian is like that too. You can tell who is following Jesus by the things they do and the things they don't do.

"Whoever says that he lives in God must live as Jesus lived," the Bible says (1 John 2:6). That means we should be kind and helpful and friendly, like Jesus was. Because Jesus was never selfish, we shouldn't be selfish either. We should think about others first, just as He did.

Because we love Jesus, we want to do only the things that will make us more like Him. Sometimes people wear wild or strange clothes or jewelry just to get attention. But the Bible says, "It is not fancy hair, gold jewelry, or fine clothes that should make you beautiful. No, your beauty should come from within you—the beauty of a gentle and quiet spirit that will never be destroyed and is very precious to God" (1 Peter 3:3, 4).

Christians are careful about what they eat and drink because they want to take care of the body God has given them. Things like dangerous drugs, alcohol, and tobacco would make us unhealthy and keep us from hearing God's voice in our hearts. We try to get plenty of exercise and eat lots of the wonderful fruits and vegetables God created.

Christians love to have fun, but not the kind of fun that hurts other people or the kind that leads us away from Jesus. We want the things that make us laugh to be the kinds of things that would make Jesus laugh. We want whatever we watch or read or hear to make us more like Jesus.

Teaching Tips

1. Make up a can you guess my pet? game. Have each child tell three things about a pet (past or present), and see if the others can guess what kind of animal it is.

2. Ask, What kinds of things make a person beautiful? Have the children draw a picture of someone who is beautiful (or handsome) the way Jesus is. Have them focus on what the person would be doing and saying rather than on what the person looks like.

3. Place a variety of items in a box or bag and have each child reach in blindly to pull one out. As they do, ask, Is this item good for us or bad for us? Why? Include such items as an orange, an apple, a carrot, a cucumber, a cigarette box, a beer can, a jogging shoe (symbolizing exercise), a jump rope (exercise), and a pillow (no exercise [bad]—or sleep [good]!).

Summary

You can tell who is following Jesus by the way they act. We should be kind and friendly and helpful like Jesus was. We take care of our bodies because they are a gift from God.

Home and Family

Bible Verse

The Lord God said, "It is not good for the man to be alone. I will make a helper who is right for him."

— Genesis 2:18

How many people are in your family? I grew up in a family with one father, one mother, two sisters, and two brothers. So there were seven people in my family.

Some of you may have only two or three in your family. Some may have nine or ten. Whatever size family you have, whether you have brothers or sisters and a father or a mother or both at home, God wants your home to be one of the happiest places in the world.

When God finished creating the world, everything was good. There were big trees full of green leaves, and that was good. There were clean rivers filled with shiny fish, and that was good. The fields were full of deer and horses and elephants, and that was good. The forests were full of monkeys and parrots and raccoons and squirrels, and that was good. God created many different kinds of animals, but He created only two people—one man and one woman. And that was good.

Instead of creating a lot of people, God created marriage and started the first family. He wanted Adam and Eve to love each other and to be together forever. He said, "Start a family. Have lots of kids. Fill the earth with people."

And Adam and Eve did that. Their children and grandchildren and great-grandchildren spread all over the world. And God blessed each marriage. Each happy family was a special gift from Him.

God still loves families. He still wants mothers and father to love each other and their children. When two people get married, they make a promise to each other and to God, and they keep that promise when they stay together and love each other. They should love each other the way Jesus loves all those who follow Him.

God wants happy families in which each person feels safe and loved. At home in a loving family, we learn more about God and His love than we do anywhere else. When we learn to obey our parents, we are learning to obey God. The Bible says, "Children, obey your parents the way the Lord wants, because this is the right thing to do" (Ephesians 6:1). And God wants parents to teach their children with love. "Fathers, do not make your children angry, but raise them with the training and teaching of the Lord" (verse 4).

By teaching their children about God, parents prepare them to join the church, God's big family.

Teaching Tips

1. Play this game: Time the children to see how long it takes them to line up in order of family size, from largest family to smallest. You'll have to decide if that means everyone who lives in the house or only mothers, fathers, sisters, and brothers.

2. Ask, What's something special your family does together? Why do you like it?

3. Have the children draw pictures of their families. Across the top of the page write God loves families.

Summary

God loves families. From Adam and Eve to today, He wants parents to stay together and love each other all their lives. He wants them to have a home where everyone feels safe and loved.

Jesus' Special Work in Heaven

Bible Verse

This is what God has told us: God has given us eternal life, and this life is in his Son. Whoever has the Son has life.

— 1 John 5:11, 12

Have you ever won a contest? When I was in third grade, we were supposed to make a poster that showed how animals made our lives better. Since we had cows on our farm, I drew a picture of a cow, then pasted on pictures of all the things cows give us—milk for ice cream and cheese, leather for boots and footballs, and calves for pets.

The judges—the people who would decide which posters were the best—looked at every poster. I won first prize! I got a nice award that my mom framed and hung on the wall, and I got ten dollars to spend on anything I wanted.

When Jesus returned to heaven, He had a special work to do. I think maybe He gathered up all the pictures He had of Himself and sat down with the Big Book of Everyone in the World. Whenever someone on earth decided to believe in Him and follow Him and learn to be like Him, Jesus would take a picture of Himself and paste it on that person's page in the Big Book. Then He could protect His followers from the bad things Satan said about them.

"Look," Satan would say, "Peter, James, and John were fighting with each other today. They're bad people. They don't deserve to come to heaven and live forever."

But Jesus would say to His Father, "Let's look at the Big Book." And when He opened the book to Peter's page, there was Jesus' picture! "The person I see here does deserve to come to heaven," God the Father would say.

Jesus does the same thing for us when we decide to believe in Him and follow Him. He puts His picture on our page in the Big Book. But the exciting thing is that when we follow Jesus and learn to be more like Him, our pictures will look more and more like His!

Before Jesus returns again, He will do another special work. Just as the judges in my poster contest looked at each poster, so Jesus will look at the life of every person who has ever lived. He'll see everything we have ever done at home, at school, and everywhere else.

But if you and I have decided to follow Jesus, His picture will be pasted on our pages. Jesus will hold up the pages with our names on them and say, "These people deserve to live in heaven. See?" And the Father will see Jesus' picture on the pages and smile.

Jesus said, "Listen! I am coming soon! I will bring my reward with me" (Revelation 22:12). All the judging will be done before Jesus returns. And everyone who has chosen Him will be saved and happy to greet the Savior.

Teaching Tips

1. Have a contest similar to the one above. Have the children draw something that shows how animals make our lives better.

2. Make a big book. You'll need photos of each child, multiple copies of an image of Jesus' face, and a big binder. Ask the children to bring a photo from home or take digital photos and print them. Assign each child to create their page for the big book by pasting their photo in place and writing around it all the things they do to be like Jesus each day. Ask, When God looks at the Big Book in heaven, what do we want Him to see? Then hand out the copies of Jesus' face that they can paste on their pages. Put all their pages in the binder, and keep the binder in their Sabbath School room.

Summary

In heaven, Jesus takes our side when Satan accuses us of being sinful. "I died for that person," Jesus says. And as long as we keep following Him, He keeps taking our side. Before Jesus comes again, He'll judge everyone who ever lived so He can decide who will live with Him forever.

Jesus Is Coming Back

Bible Verse

"After I go and prepare a place for you, I will come back and take you to be with me so that you may be where I am."

— John 14:3

Is it cold in winter where you live? Do you have snow or ice storms? I like snow, but I wouldn't like to shovel it off my driveway all year long!

It's almost spring where I live. Do you know how I can tell? It's getter warmer in the afternoons. It stays light longer every evening. I've seen robins hopping across the lawn looking for bugs. And today, I saw a bright yellow daffodil poking up out of the ground!

Spring is coming. I know because I see the signs of spring every day.

Before Jesus went to heaven, He made a promise. He said, "There are many rooms in my Father's house. . . . I am going there to prepare a place for you. After I go and prepare a place for you, I will come back and take you to be with me so that you may be where I am" (John 14:2, 3).

But when will Jesus come again? Jesus said, "You will hear about wars and stories of wars that are coming, but don't be afraid. These things must happen before the end comes. . . . There will be times when there is no food for people to eat, and there will be earthquakes in different places" (Matthew 24:6, 7).

Jesus also said that there will be more and more evil in the world and that people will stop caring about each other. But the most important sign of all is this:

"The Good News about God's kingdom will be preached in all the world, to every nation. Then the end will come" (Matthew 24:14).

We know that Jesus will return soon because we can see the signs. There are wars, and many people have almost no food to eat. Earthquakes and deadly storms happen more and more. And today, the good news about God's love is being preached in almost every country. It seems that Jesus is going to keep His promise very soon!

And when Jesus returns, no one will miss it! The Bible says that everyone in the world will see Him in the sky. His coming won't be a secret that anyone can keep. "The Lord himself will come down from heaven with a loud command, with the voice of the archangel, and with the trumpet call of God" (1 Thessalonians 4:16).

No one is going to sleep through that! Even the people who have died will wake up and join us as we rise up in the air to meet Jesus on His big white cloud! The only people who won't be happy are those who weren't looking for Jesus, who didn't want to follow Him or be like Him. They would rather die than go to heaven to be with Jesus, so God lets them die.

Even though we don't know when Jesus will return, we can still be ready to meet Him every day.

Teaching Tips

1. Depending on where you live and what time of year it is, ask the children, How do we know when the next season is coming? What are the signs?

2. Have the children create 3-D pictures or dioramas of the Second Coming. Find images of Jesus and angels that they can cut out and color. Use cotton balls to show the clouds as Jesus returns. Paste Jesus and the angels to the cotton clouds.

3. Ask, What signs do we see that Jesus is coming soon? Is that scary sometimes? Does it make you happy sometimes?

Summary

All the signs tell us that Jesus is returning soon. When He does come, everyone in the world will see Him.

What Happens When People Die

Bible Verse

The trumpet will sound, and those who have died will be raised to live forever.

— 1 Corinthians 15:52

I remember the day when my dad told us that my grandfather was very sick—so sick that he wasn't going to get better. Before long, he died. It was the first time that someone I knew died, and I wasn't sure what would happen next. That's when I learned about funerals.

Have you ever been to a funeral? A funeral is a special service, usually at church, when family and friends of someone who died gather together to remember that person. My grandfather's funeral was sad and a little scary. People were crying and singing and praying, and I was sad and confused.

It's very sad when someone dies. It's hard to understand why it happens, whether someone dies because they get sick or because they get hurt. I think it's hard to understand because God never wanted it to happen. When He created people, He planned for them to live forever and never die.

But sin came to our world when Adam and Eve chose to listen to Satan instead of to God. And when sin came into our world, so did death. Everyone who is born grows up, gets old, and dies. But God has a plan to fix everything. Jesus came to our world and died for our sins. When He comes again, He'll put an end to sin and death forever.

When a person dies, it's like they've gone to sleep. But this time, they won't wake up from their sleep until Jesus comes back again. The Bible says, "The living know that they will die, but the dead know nothing" (Ecclesiastes 9:5, NIV). Their body is buried in the ground, but God remembers them. So even though we're sad and we miss them, we don't have to be as sad as people who don't know about God—because we know that Jesus is coming back soon!

The Bible promises, "The Lord himself will come down from heaven with a loud command, with the voice of the archangel, and with the trumpet call of God. And those who have died believing in Christ will rise first. After that, those who are still alive will be gathered up with them in the clouds to meet the Lord in the air" (1 Thessalonians 4:16, 17).

When the angels blow those trumpets, everyone who died loving Jesus will wake up from their long sleep and go home with Him.

Teaching Tips

1. Ask, Has someone you know died? A grandparent, a friend, a pet? How did that make you feel?

2. Make trumpets either by cutting out trumpet shapes from poster board or by collecting empty paper-towel rolls. Decorate the trumpets brightly with sparkles and glitter. Then, with trumpets in hand, march through the halls of the church, making trumpeting noises. Tell the children that when anyone asks what they're doing, they should say, "We're the angels who will blow the trumpets when Jesus comes!"

Summary

People die because sin came into our world. When someone dies, it's as if they've gone to sleep and they won't wake up until Jesus calls them when He returns.

The Thousand Years and the End of Sin

Bible Verse

God . . . does not want anyone to be lost, but he wants all people to change their hearts and lives.

— 2 Peter 3:9

When Jesus calls everyone who loves Him back to life and takes them to heaven, they will be free from sin and death forever. But not everyone will choose to believe in Jesus and follow Him. No matter how much God loves people, and no matter how many times He tries to talk to them, some people choose to be selfish and mean. Just like Satan, they want to ignore God's rules of life and do whatever they want even if it hurts other people.

Those people think they can live without God. But they don't understand that God's laws are keeping them alive because He is the Creator of life. And when God gets rid of sin forever, He also has to get rid of everyone who holds on to sin, everyone who refuses to follow His laws.

When Jesus returns to earth and takes the people who love Him up in the clouds, the bright light around Him destroys everything left on earth. The only things still alive in the whole world are Satan and his angels. They'll spend a thousand years thinking about the bad things they've done.

Jesus and His people spend the thousand years in heaven together. When the thousand years are over, they ride the Holy City, the New Jerusalem—their special home in heaven—back down to earth. Finally, it's time for God to put an end to sin forever.

Everyone else who ever lived—everyone who refused to follow God or live by His rules—comes back to life at this time. The Bible says that Satan will make all those people into an army. "And Satan's army marched across the earth and gathered around the camp of God's people and the city God loves. But fire came down from heaven and burned them up" (Revelation 20:9).

On that day, Satan, sin, and all the people who won't let go of sin and selfishness will be destroyed forever. The Bible says, "All the proud and evil people will be like straw. On that day they will be completely burned up" (Malachi 4:1).

And that will be the end of sin forever. The Bible says, "I heard a loud voice from the throne, saying 'Now God's presence is with people, and he will live with them, and they will be his people. God himself will be with them and will be their God. He will wipe away every tear from their eyes, and there will be no more death, sadness, crying, or pain because all the old ways are gone' " (Revelation 21:3, 4).

Teaching Tips

1. To make sure the children understand, ask, Why doesn't God just take everyone to heaven? Stress the answer that God doesn't force anyone to go, and some people don't want to be with God.

2. If possible, help the children understand the concept of a thousand by bringing in one thousand pennies for the group to count. That's twenty penny rolls of fifty coins each.

3. For a unique coloring project, say, Color a sheet of paper with all the colors you imagine there are in heaven. (No shapes or images, just colors.) Next, say, When sin came to our world, it blocked out the beauty of heaven. So, now color over your paper with solid black. When everyone is done, say, Everyone who wants to be in heaven will choose Jesus. Then have them scrape away the black with the rounded edge of a paperclip or similar object to write the words I choose Jesus and God ends sin forever plus whatever shapes or images they like.

Summary

When Jesus returns, He will take everyone who chose to believe in Him back to heaven for a thousand years. Everyone else on earth will die. After the thousand years, Jesus and His people will return to earth in the Holy City, the New Jerusalem. Then all those who hated God will come back to life and follow Satan; they'll try to attack the city. But God will destroy sin and sinners forever.

A Brand-New Earth

God made a promise to us, and we are waiting for a new heaven and a new earth where goodness lives.

— 2 Peter 3:13

Imagine you have a treehouse in your backyard. Imagine it's the kind of treehouse that has a trapdoor with a rope ladder that you can pull up inside. It's such a good treehouse that squirrels keep trying to move in every time you leave.

Then imagine that one morning your dad says, "I'm going to tear down that old treehouse. The squirrels have chewed holes in the roof, and the rope ladder is starting to break. I'm going to have to destroy that treehouse."

How would you feel? Would you jump up and down and shout "No!"? If you really loved your treehouse, only one thing would make tearing it down OK. It would be OK only if your dad added a promise: "I'm going to build you a brand-new treehouse much better than this one!"

God made a promise like that to us. The Bible says, "We are waiting for what he promised—a new heaven and a new earth where goodness lives" (see 2 Peter 3:13). This world where we live is getting old. Plants and animals get sick and die. The mountains and rivers and forests are pretty, but not nearly as nice as they were when God created them.

And the people are different too. God created perfect humans who would never get sick or old. Today people get hurt in car crashes and wars. They get sick with the flu and with cancer. They are often sad and lonely or mean and selfish.

When Jesus comes back, He'll change every person who chooses to live with Him into a brand-new person. None of them will ever get sick or cry. And when sin is finally destroyed, Jesus will make a new earth for His people. It will be their home forever. It will be better than the old world because there won't be anything to make people sick—no poison ivy, no allergies, and no mosquitoes that bite.

The new world will be a different kind of place. The Bible says,

> *"Wolves and lambs will eat together in peace.*
> *Lions will eat hay like oxen,*
> *and a snake on the ground will not hurt anyone.*
> *They will not hurt or destroy each other."* — Isaiah 65:25

But best of all, Jesus will live there with us. And He'll answer all the questions in the universe. If we ask, "What is the farthest place from earth?" or "How many stars are there, really?" He'll know the answers. If we ask, "Where do rainbows go when they disappear?" or "What lives at the bottom of the ocean?" He'll tell us.

And sin will never be a problem again. Everyone and everything in the universe will know that God is love, and they will want to live with Him forever.

Teaching Tips

1. Share a treehouse story if you have one, or ask, What kind of treehouse would you have if you could choose?

2. Ask, What questions do you want to ask Jesus when you live with Him on the new earth?

3. Have the children draw a picture of themselves in the new world. Ask what they will be doing: Riding a giraffe? Flying over a mountain? Walking around on the bottom of the ocean?

Summary

With sin gone forever, Jesus will create a new earth as perfect as the Garden of Eden. Then He will live there with us forever.

Fundamental Beliefs of the Seventh-day Adventist Church

Seventh-day Adventists accept the Bible as their only creed and hold certain fundamental beliefs to be the teachings of the Holy Scriptures. These beliefs, as set forth here, constitute the church's understanding and expression of the teaching of Scripture. Revision of these statements may be expected at a General Conference session when the church is led by the Holy Spirit to a fuller understanding of Bible truths or finds better language to express the teachings of God's Holy Word.

1. The Holy Scriptures

The Holy Scriptures, Old and New Testaments, are the written Word of God, given by divine inspiration through holy men of God who spoke and wrote as they were moved by the Holy Spirit. In this Word, God has committed to man the knowledge necessary for salvation. The Holy Scriptures are the infallible revelation of His will. They are the standard of character, the test of experience, the authoritative revealer of doctrines, and the trustworthy record of God's acts in history.

(2 Pet. 1:20, 21; 2 Tim. 3:16, 17; Ps. 119:105; Prov. 30:5, 6; Isa. 8:20; John 17:17; 1 Thess. 2:13; Heb. 4:12.)

2. The Trinity

There is one God: Father, Son, and Holy Spirit, a unity of three co-eternal Persons. God is immortal, all-powerful, all-knowing, above all, and ever present. He is infinite and beyond human comprehension, yet known through His self-revelation. He is forever worthy of worship, adoration, and service by the whole creation.

(Deut. 6:4; Matt. 28:19; 2 Cor. 13:14; Eph. 4:4–6; 1 Peter 1:2; 1 Tim. 1:17; Rev. 14:7.)

3. The Father

God the eternal Father is the Creator, Source, Sustainer, and Sovereign of all creation. He is just and holy, merciful and gracious, slow to anger, and abounding in steadfast love and faithfulness. The qualities and powers exhibited in the Son and the Holy Spirit are also revelations of the Father.

(Gen. 1:1; Rev. 4:11; 1 Cor. 15:28; John 3:16; 1 John 4:8; 1 Tim. 1:17; Exod. 34:6, 7; John 14:9.)

4. The Son

God the eternal Son became incarnate in Jesus Christ. Through Him all things were created, the character of God is revealed, the salvation of humanity is accomplished, and the world is judged. Forever truly God, He became also truly man, Jesus the Christ. He was conceived of the Holy Spirit and born of the virgin Mary. He lived and experienced temptation as a human being, but perfectly exemplified the righteousness and love of God. By His miracles He manifested God's power and was attested as God's promised Messiah. He suffered and died voluntarily on the cross for our sins and in our place, was raised from the dead, and ascended to minister in the heavenly sanctuary in our behalf. He will come again in glory for the final deliverance of His people and the restoration of all things.

(John 1:1–3, 14; Col. 1:15–19; John 10:30; 14:9; Rom. 6:23; 2 Cor. 5:17–19; John 5:22; Luke 1:35; Phil. 2:5–11; Heb. 2:9–18; 1 Cor. 15:3, 4; Heb. 8:1, 2; John 14:1–3.)

5. The Holy Spirit

God the eternal Spirit was active with the Father and the Son in Creation, incarnation, and redemption. He inspired the writers of Scripture. He filled Christ's life with power. He draws and convicts human beings; and those who respond He renews and transforms into the image of God. Sent by the Father and the Son to be always with His children, He extends spiritual gifts to the church, empowers it to bear witness to Christ, and in harmony with the Scriptures leads it into all truth.

(Gen. 1:1, 2; Luke 1:35; 4:18; Acts 10:38; 2 Pet. 1:21; 2 Cor. 3:18; Eph. 4:11, 12; Acts 1:8; John 14:16–18, 26; 15:26, 27; 16:7–13.)

6. Creation

God is Creator of all things, and has revealed in Scripture the authentic account of His creative activity. In six days the Lord made "the heaven and the earth" and all living things upon the earth, and rested on the seventh day of that first week. Thus He established the Sabbath as a perpetual memorial of His completed creative work. The first man and woman were made in the image of God as the crowning work of Creation, given dominion over the world, and charged with responsibility to care for it. When the world was finished it was "very good," declaring the glory of God.

(Gen. 1; 2; Exod. 20:8–11; Pss. 19:1–6; 33:6, 9; 104; Heb. 11:3.)

7. The Nature of Man

Man and woman were made in the image of God with individuality, the power and freedom to think and to do. Though created free beings, each is an indivisible unity of body, mind, and spirit, dependent upon God for life and breath and all else. When our first parents disobeyed God, they denied their dependence upon Him and fell from their high position under God. The image of God in them was marred and they became subject to death. Their descendants share this fallen nature and its consequences. They are born with weaknesses and tendencies to evil. But God in Christ reconciled the world to Himself and by His Spirit restores in penitent mortals the image of their Maker. Created for the glory of God, they are called to love Him and one another, and to care for their environment.

(Gen. 1:26–28; 2:7; Ps. 8:4–8; Acts 17:24–28; Gen. 3; Ps. 51:5; Rom. 5:12–17; 2 Cor. 5:19, 20; Ps. 51:10; 1 John 4:7, 8, 11, 20; Gen. 2:15.)

8. The Great Controversy

All humanity is now involved in a great controversy between Christ and Satan regarding the character of God, His law, and His sovereignty over the universe. This conflict originated in heaven when a created being, endowed with freedom of choice, in self-exaltation became Satan, God's adversary, and led into rebellion a portion of the angels. He introduced the spirit of rebellion into this world when he led Adam and Eve into sin. This human sin resulted in the distortion of the image of God in humanity, the disordering of the created world, and its eventual devastation at the time of the worldwide flood. Observed by the whole creation, this world became the arena of the universal conflict, out of which the God of love will ultimately be vindicated. To assist His people in this controversy, Christ sends the Holy Spirit and the loyal angels to guide, protect, and sustain them in the way of salvation.

(Rev. 12:4–9; Isa. 14:12–14; Ezek. 28:12-18; Gen. 3; Rom. 1:19–32; 5:12–21; 8:19–22; Gen. 6–8; 2 Pet. 3:6; 1 Cor. 4:9; Heb. 1:14.)

9. The Life, Death, and Resurrection of Christ

In Christ's life of perfect obedience to God's will, His suffering, death, and resurrection, God provided the only means of atonement for human sin, so that those who by faith accept this atonement may have eternal life, and the whole creation may better understand the infinite and holy love of the Creator. This perfect atonement vindicates the righteousness of God's law and the graciousness of His character; for it both condemns our sin and provides for our forgiveness. The death of Christ is substitutionary and expiatory, reconciling and transforming. The resurrection of Christ proclaims God's triumph over the forces of evil, and for those who accept the atonement assures their final victory over sin and death. It declares the Lordship of Jesus Christ, before whom every knee in heaven and on earth will bow.

(John 3:16; Isa. 53; 1 Pet. 2:21, 22; 1 Cor. 15:3, 4, 20–22; 2 Cor. 5:14, 15, 19–21; Rom. 1:4; 3:25; 4:25; 8:3, 4; 1 John 2:2; 4:10; Col. 2:15; Phil. 2:6–11.)

10. The Experience of Salvation

In infinite love and mercy God made Christ, who knew no sin, to be sin for us, so that in Him we might be made the righteousness of God. Led by the Holy Spirit we sense our need, acknowledge our sinfulness, repent of our transgressions, and exercise faith in Jesus as Lord and Christ, as Substitute and Example. This faith which receives salvation comes through the divine power of the Word and is the gift of God's grace. Through Christ we are justified, adopted as God's sons and daughters, and delivered from the lordship of sin. Through the Spirit we are born again and sanctified; the Spirit renews our minds, writes God's law of love in our hearts, and we are given the power to live a holy life. Abiding in Him we become partakers of the divine nature and have the assurance of salvation now and in the judgment.

(2 Cor. 5:17–21; John 3:16; Gal. 1:4; 4:4–7; Titus 3:3–7; John 16:8; Gal. 3:13, 14; 1 Pet. 2:21, 22; Rom. 10:17; Luke 17:5; Mark 9:23, 24; Eph. 2:5–10; Rom. 3:21–26; Col. 1:13, 14; Rom. 8:14–17; Gal. 3:26; John 3:3–8; 1 Pet. 1:23; Rom. 12:2; Heb. 8:7–12; Ezek. 36:25–27; 2 Pet. 1:3, 4; Rom. 8:1–4; 5:6–10.)

11. Growing in Christ

By His death on the cross Jesus triumphed over the forces of evil. He who subjugated the demonic spirits during His earthly ministry has broken their power and made certain their ultimate doom. Jesus' victory gives us victory over the evil forces that still seek to control us, as we walk with Him in peace, joy, and assurance of His love. Now the Holy Spirit dwells within us and empowers us. Continually committed to Jesus as our Saviour and Lord, we are set free from the burden of our past deeds. No longer do we live in the darkness, fear of evil powers, ignorance, and meaninglessness of our former way of life. In this new freedom in Jesus, we are called to grow into the likeness of His character, communing with Him daily in prayer, feeding on His Word, meditating on it and on His providence, singing His praises, gathering together for worship, and participating in the mission of the church. As we give ourselves in loving service to those around us and in witnessing to His salvation, His constant presence with us through the Spirit transforms every moment and every task into a spiritual experience.

(Pss. 1:1, 2; 23:4; 77:11, 12; Col. 1:13, 14; 2:6, 14, 15; Luke 10:17–20; Eph. 5:19, 20; 6:12–18; 1 Thess. 5:23; 2 Pet. 2:9; 3:18; 2 Cor. 3:17, 18; Phil. 3:7–14; 1 Thess. 5:16–18; Matt. 20:25–28; John 20:21; Gal. 5:22–25; Rom. 8:38, 39; 1 John 4:4; Heb. 10:25.)

12. The Church

The church is the community of believers who confess Jesus Christ as Lord and Saviour. In continuity with the people of God in Old Testament times, we are called out from the world; and we join together for worship, for fellowship, for instruction in the Word, for the celebration of the Lord's

Supper, for service to all mankind, and for the worldwide proclamation of the gospel. The church derives its authority from Christ, who is the incarnate Word, and from the Scriptures, which are the written Word. The church is God's family; adopted by Him as children, its members live on the basis of the new covenant. The church is the body of Christ, a community of faith of which Christ Himself is the Head. The church is the bride for whom Christ died that He might sanctify and cleanse her. At His return in triumph, He will present her to Himself a glorious church, the faithful of all the ages, the purchase of His blood, not having spot or wrinkle, but holy and without blemish.

(Gen. 12:3; Acts 7:38; Eph. 4:11–15; 3:8–11; Matt. 28:19, 20; 16:13–20; 18:18; Eph. 2:19–22; 1:22, 23; 5:23–27; Col. 1:17, 18.)

13. The Remnant and Its Mission

The universal church is composed of all who truly believe in Christ, but in the last days, a time of widespread apostasy, a remnant has been called out to keep the commandments of God and the faith of Jesus. This remnant announces the arrival of the judgment hour, proclaims salvation through Christ, and heralds the approach of His second advent. This proclamation is symbolized by the three angels of Revelation 14; it coincides with the work of judgment in heaven and results in a work of repentance and reform on earth. Every believer is called to have a personal part in this worldwide witness.

(Rev. 12:17; 14:6–12; 18:1–4; 2 Cor. 5:10; Jude 3, 14; 1 Pet. 1:16–19; 2 Pet. 3:10–14; Rev. 21:1–14.)

14. Unity in the Body of Christ

The church is one body with many members, called from every nation, kindred, tongue, and people. In Christ we are a new creation; distinctions of race, culture, learning, and nationality, and differences between high and low, rich and poor, male and female, must not be divisive among us. We are all equal in Christ, who by one Spirit has bonded us into one fellowship with Him and with one another; we are to serve and be served without partiality or reservation. Through the revelation of Jesus Christ in the Scriptures we share the same faith and hope, and reach out in one witness to all. This unity has its source in the oneness of the triune God, who has adopted us as His children.

(Rom. 12:4, 5; 1 Cor. 12:12–14; Matt. 28:19, 20; Ps. 133:1; 2 Cor. 5:16, 17; Acts 17:26, 27; Gal. 3:27, 29; Col. 3:10–15; Eph. 4:14–16; 4:1–6; John 17:20–23.)

15. Baptism

By baptism we confess our faith in the death and resurrection of Jesus Christ, and testify of our death to sin and of our purpose to walk in newness of life. Thus we acknowledge Christ as Lord and Saviour, become His people, and are received as members by His church. Baptism is a symbol of our union with Christ, the forgiveness of our sins, and our reception of the Holy Spirit. It is by immersion in water and is contingent on an affirmation of faith in Jesus and evidence of repentance of sin. It follows instruction in the Holy Scriptures and acceptance of their teachings.

(Rom. 6:1–6; Col. 2:12, 13; Acts 16:30–33; 22:16; 2:38; Matt. 28:19, 20.)

16. The Lord's Supper

The Lord's Supper is a participation in the emblems of the body and blood of Jesus as an expression of faith in Him, our Lord and Saviour. In this experience of communion Christ is present to meet and strengthen His people. As we partake, we joyfully proclaim the Lord's death until He comes again. Preparation for the Supper includes self-examination, repentance, and confession. The Master ordained the service of foot washing to signify renewed cleansing, to express a willingness to serve one another in Christlike humility, and to unite our hearts in love. The communion service is open to all believing Christians.

(1 Cor. 10:16, 17; 11:23–30; Matt. 26:17–30; Rev. 3:20; John 6:48–63; 13:1–17.)

17. Spiritual Gifts and Ministries

God bestows upon all members of His church in every age spiritual gifts which each member is to employ in loving ministry for the common good of the church and of humanity. Given by the agency of the Holy Spirit, who apportions to each member as He wills, the gifts provide all abilities and ministries needed by the church to fulfill its divinely ordained functions. According to the Scriptures, these gifts include such ministries as faith, healing, prophecy, proclamation, teaching, administration, reconciliation, compassion, and self-sacrificing service and charity for the help and encouragement of people. Some members are called of God and endowed by the Spirit for functions recognized by the church in pastoral, evangelistic, apostolic, and teaching ministries particularly needed to equip the members for service, to build up the church to spiritual maturity, and to foster unity of the faith and knowledge of God. When members employ these spiritual gifts as faithful stewards of God's varied grace, the church is protected from the destructive influence of false doctrine, grows with a growth that is from God, and is built up in faith and love.

(Rom. 12:4–8; 1 Cor. 12:9–11, 27, 28; Eph. 4:8, 11–16; Acts 6:1–7; 1 Tim. 3:1–13; 1 Pet. 4:10, 11.)

18. The Gift of Prophecy

One of the gifts of the Holy Spirit is prophecy. This gift is an identifying mark of the remnant church and was manifested in the ministry of Ellen. G. White. As the Lord's messenger, her writings are a continuing and authoritative source of truth which provide for the church comfort, guidance, instruction, and correction. They also make clear that the Bible is the standard by which all teaching and experience must be tested.

(Joel 2:28, 29; Acts 2:14–21; Heb. 1:1–3; Rev. 12:17; 19:10.)

19. The Law of God

The great principles of God's law are embodied in the Ten Commandments and exemplified in the life of Christ. They express God's love, will, and purposes concerning human conduct and relationships and are binding upon all people in every age. These precepts are the basis of God's covenant with His people and the standard in God's judgment. Through the agency of the Holy Spirit they point out sin and awaken a sense of need for a Saviour. Salvation is all of grace and not of works, but its fruitage is obedience to the Commandments. This obedience develops Christian character and results in a sense of well-being. It is an evidence of our love for the Lord and our concern for our fellow men. The obedience of faith demonstrates the power of Christ to transform lives, and therefore strengthens Christian witness.

(Exod. 20:1–17; Ps. 40:7, 8; Matt. 22:36–40; Deut. 28:1–14; Matt. 5:17–20; Heb. 8:8–10; John 15:7–10; Eph. 2:8–10; 1 John 5:3; Rom. 8:3, 4; Ps. 19:7–14.)

20. The Sabbath

The beneficent Creator, after the six days of Creation, rested on the seventh day and instituted the Sabbath for all people as a memorial of Creation. The fourth commandment of God's unchangeable law requires the observance of this seventh-day Sabbath as the day of rest, worship, and ministry in harmony with the teaching and practice of Jesus, the Lord of the Sabbath. The Sabbath is a day of delightful communion with God and one another. It is a symbol of our redemption in Christ, a sign of our sanctification, a token of our allegiance, and a foretaste of our eternal future in God's kingdom. The Sabbath is God's perpetual sign of His eternal covenant between Him and His people. Joyful observance of this holy time from evening to evening, sunset to sunset, is a celebration of God's creative and redemptive acts.

(Gen. 2:1–3; Exod. 20:8–11; Luke 4:16; Isa. 56:5, 6; 58:13, 14; Matt. 12:1–12; Exod. 31:13–17; Ezek. 20:12, 20; Deut. 5:12–15; Heb. 4:1–11; Lev. 23:32; Mark 1:32.)

21. Stewardship

We are God's stewards, entrusted by Him with time and opportunities, abilities and possessions, and the blessings of the earth and its resources. We are responsible to Him for their proper use. We acknowledge God's ownership by faithful service to Him and our fellow men, and by returning tithes and giving offerings for the proclamation of His gospel and the support and growth of His church. Stewardship is a privilege given to us by God for nurture in love and the victory over selfishness and covetousness. The steward rejoices in the blessings that come to others as a result of his faithfulness.

(Gen. 1:26–28; 2:15; 1 Chron. 29:14; Hag. 1:3–11; Mal. 3:8–12; 1 Cor. 9:9–14; Matt. 23:23; 2 Cor. 8:1–15; Rom. 15:26, 27.)

22. Christian Behavior

We are called to be a godly people who think, feel, and act in harmony with the principles of heaven. For the Spirit to recreate in us the character of our Lord we involve ourselves only in those things which will produce Christlike purity, health, and joy in our lives. This means that our amusement and entertainment should meet the highest standards of Christian taste and beauty. While recognizing cultural differences, our dress is to be simple, modest, and neat, befitting those whose true beauty does not consist of outward adornment but in the imperishable ornament of a gentle and quiet spirit. It also means that because our bodies are the temples of the Holy Spirit, we are to care for them intelligently. Along with adequate exercise and rest, we are to adopt the most healthful diet possible and abstain from the unclean foods identified in the Scriptures. Since alcoholic beverages, tobacco, and the irresponsible use of drugs and narcotics are harmful to our bodies, we are to abstain from them as well. Instead, we are to engage in whatever brings our thoughts and bodies into the discipline of Christ, who desires our wholesomeness, joy, and goodness.

(Rom. 12:1, 2; 1 John 2:6; Eph. 5:1–21; Phil. 4:8; 2 Cor. 10:5; 6:14–7:1; 1 Pet. 3:1–4; 1 Cor. 6:19, 20; 10:31; Lev. 11:1–47; 3 John 2.)

23. Marriage and the Family

Marriage was divinely established in Eden and affirmed by Jesus to be a lifelong union between a man and a woman in loving companionship. For the Christian a marriage commitment is to God as well as to the spouse, and should be entered into only between partners who share a common faith. Mutual love, honor, respect, and responsibility are the fabric of this relationship, which is to reflect the love, sanctity, closeness, and permanence of the relationship between Christ and His church. Regarding divorce, Jesus taught that the person who divorces a spouse, except for fornication, and marries another, commits adultery. Although some family relationships may fall short of the ideal, marriage partners who fully commit themselves to each other in Christ may achieve loving unity through the guidance of the Spirit and the nurture of the church. God blesses the family and intends that its members shall assist each other toward complete maturity. Parents are to bring up their children to love and obey the Lord. By their example and their words they are to teach them that Christ is a loving disciplinarian, ever tender and caring, who wants them to become members of His body, the family of God. Increasing family closeness is one of the earmarks of the final gospel message.

(Gen. 2:18–25; Matt. 19:3–9; John 2:1–11; 2 Cor. 6:14; Eph. 5:21–33; Matt. 5:31, 32; Mark 10:11, 12; Luke 16:18; 1 Cor. 7:10, 11; Exod. 20:12; Eph. 6:1–4; Deut. 6:5–9; Prov. 22:6; Mal. 4:5, 6.)

24. Christ's Ministry in the Heavenly Sanctuary

There is a sanctuary in heaven, the true tabernacle which the Lord set up and not man. In it Christ ministers on our behalf, making available to believers the benefits of His atoning sacrifice offered once for all on the cross. He was inaugurated as our great High Priest and began His intercessory ministry at the time of His ascension. In 1844, at the end of the prophetic period of 2300 days, He entered the second and last phase of His atoning ministry. It is a work of investigative judgment which is part of the ultimate disposition of all sin, typified by the cleansing of the ancient Hebrew sanctuary on the Day of Atonement. In that typical service the sanctuary was cleansed with the blood of animal sacrifices, but the heavenly things are purified with the perfect sacrifice of the blood of Jesus. The investigative judgment reveals to heavenly intelligences who among the dead are asleep in Christ and therefore, in Him, are deemed worthy to have part in the first resurrection. It also makes manifest who among the living are abiding in Christ, keeping the commandments of God and the faith of Jesus, and in Him, therefore, are ready for translation into His everlasting kingdom. This judgment vindicates the justice of God in saving those who believe in Jesus. It declares that those who have remained loyal to God shall receive the kingdom. The completion of this ministry of Christ will mark the close of human probation before the Second Advent.

(Heb. 8:1–5; 4:14–16; 9:11–28; 10:19–22; 1:3; 2:16, 17; Dan. 7:9–27; 8:13, 14; 9:24–27; Num. 14:34; Ezek. 4:6; Lev. 16; Rev. 14:6, 7; 20:12; 14:12; 22:12.)

25. The Second Coming of Christ

The second coming of Christ is the blessed hope of the church, the grand climax of the gospel. The Saviour's coming will be literal, personal, visible, and worldwide. When He returns, the righteous dead will be resurrected, and together with the righteous living will be glorified and taken to heaven, but the unrighteous will die. The almost complete fulfillment of most lines of prophecy, together with the present condition of the world, indicates that Christ's coming is imminent. The time of that event has not been revealed, and we are therefore exhorted to be ready at all times.

(Titus 2:13; Heb. 9:28; John 14:1–3; Acts 1:9–11; Matt. 24:14; Rev. 1:7; Matt. 24:43, 44; 1 Thess. 4:13–18; 1 Cor. 15:51–54; 2 Thess. 1:7–10; 2:8; Rev. 14:14–20; 19:11–21; Matt. 24; Mark 13; Luke 21; 2 Tim. 3:1-5; 1 Thess. 5:1–6.)

26. Death and Resurrection

The wages of sin is death. But God, who alone is immortal, will grant eternal life to His redeemed. Until that day death is an unconscious state for all people. When Christ, who is our life, appears, the resurrected righteous and the living righteous will be glorified and caught up to meet their Lord. The second resurrection, the resurrection of the unright–eous, will take place a thousand years later.

(Rom. 6:23; 1 Tim. 6:15, 16; Eccles. 9:5, 6; Ps. 146:3, 4; John 11:11–14; Col. 3:4; 1 Cor. 15:51–54; 1 Thess. 4:13–17; John 5:28, 29; Rev. 20:1–10.)

27. The Millennium and the End of Sin

The millennium is the thousand-year reign of Christ with His saints in heaven between the first and second resurrections. During this time the wicked dead will be judged; the earth will be utterly desolate, without living human inhabitants, but occupied by Satan and his angels. At its close Christ with His saints and the Holy City will descend from heaven to earth. The unrighteous dead will then be resurrected, and with Satan and his angels will surround the city; but fire from God will consume them and cleanse the earth. The universe will thus be freed of sin and sinners forever.

(Rev. 20; 1 Cor. 6:2, 3; Jer. 4:23–26; Rev. 21:1–5; Mal. 4:1; Ezek. 28:18, 19.)

28. The New Earth

On the new earth, in which righteousness dwells, God will provide an eternal home for the redeemed and a perfect environment for everlasting life, love, joy, and learning in His presence. For here God Himself will dwell with His people, and suffering and death will have passed away. The great controversy will be ended, and sin will be no more. All things, animate and inanimate, will declare that God is love; and He shall reign forever. Amen.

(2 Pet. 3:13; Isa. 35; 65:17–25; Matt. 5:5; Rev. 21:1–7; 22:1–5; 11:15.)

STUCK ON THE PRESIDENTS

Sticker art by Kathie Kelleher
Written by Lara Bergen, Lisa Hopp, and Angela Tung

GROSSET & DUNLAP
Published by the Penguin Group
Penguin Group (USA) Inc., 375 Hudson Street, New York, New York 10014, USA
Penguin Group (Canada), 90 Eglinton Avenue East, Suite 700, Toronto,
Ontario M4P 2Y3, Canada
(a division of Pearson Penguin Canada Inc.)
Penguin Books Ltd., 80 Strand, London WC2R 0RL, England
Penguin Group Ireland, 25 St. Stephen's Green, Dublin 2, Ireland
(a division of Penguin Books Ltd.)
Penguin Group (Australia), 250 Camberwell Road, Camberwell, Victoria 3124, Australia
(a division of Pearson Australia Group Pty. Ltd.)
Penguin Books India Pvt. Ltd., 11 Community Centre,
Panchsheel Park, New Delhi—110 017, India
Penguin Group (NZ), 67 Apollo Drive, Rosedale, North Shore 0632, New Zealand
(a division of Pearson New Zealand Ltd.)
Penguin Books (South Africa) (Pty.) Ltd., 24 Sturdee Avenue,
Rosebank, Johannesburg 2196, South Africa

Penguin Books Ltd., Registered Offices: 80 Strand, London WC2R 0RL, England

ISBN 978-0-448-44980-7   10 9 8 7 6 5 4 3 2 1

THE PRESIDENTIAL OATH OF OFFICE

"I do solemnly swear
that I will faithfully execute
the office of President of the United States,
and will to the best of my ability,
preserve, protect, and defend
the Constitution of the United States."

Only a select number of people have gotten to recite these words. What did they all have in common? They all had the same title: **President of the United States**. Some were born in mansions, others in log cabins, Some went to fancy schools. Others taught themselves to read. But they were all elected to do the same job: lead the country.

The job of the president is many jobs rolled into one:

- As **Chief Executive**, the president is the head of the executive branch of the government, and in charge of nominating judges, ambassadors, and other government officials.

- As **Commander in Chief**, the president is the leader of the Army, Navy, Air Force, and Marines.

- As **Foreign Policy Director**, the president guides U.S. relations with other nations.

- As **Legislative Leader**, the president proposes new laws to Congress.

- As **Chief of State**, the president presides over official ceremonies and is the leader of the American people.

Now that you know what all presidents have in common, let's find out what makes each one special....

GEORGE WASHINGTON

President from **1789–1797**

George Washington was so popular, many people wanted to crown him *king*! But George would have no part of it. Instead, he was elected president—the very first!

Martha Washington
What should people call the *first* first lady? "Lady Washington," "Mrs. President," or "Presidentress"? Down-to-earth Martha preferred plain old "Mrs. Washington."

Washington was the only president who never lived in the White House.

1732 - 1799

We cannot tell a lie— the Father of Our Country never did chop down a cherry tree. The story was started after his death.

North Carolina, Vermont, Kentucky, and *Tennessee* became states.

 Washington had just one real tooth when he became president. His false teeth were made from cow's teeth and hippo bone.

 In 1793, Washington put down the cornerstone for the U.S. Capitol.

1789	1790	1791	1792	1793	1794	1795	1796	1797

Washington is sworn in

First American ship sails around the world

Washington chooses site of the new nation's capital

Construction begins on the White House

Washington is reelected

First hotel in the U.S. opens

John Adams defeats Thomas Jefferson in presidential election

3

Find the Washington stickers on sticker page A.

JOHN ADAMS

Like Washington, Adams didn't have many teeth left when he became president, but he refused to wear dentures and so spoke with a lisp. Adams was the first president who had a son who became president, too.

Abigail Smith Adams
Abigail Adams was the first first lady to be the wife of one president and mother of another—John Quincy Adams. She was also an early supporter of women's rights.

Adams and Jefferson were the only two signers of the Declaration of Independence to become president— and both died on the fiftieth anniversary of its signing!

1735 - 1826

In 1800, Adams started the Library of Congress.

Mississippi and *Indiana* became territories.

Adams hurried to build a strong navy to protect American ships from countries like England and France. The first naval ship, the *United States*, set sail in 1797.

In November 1800, Adams and his family moved into the brand-new White House— or at least into the six rooms that were finished.

1797	1798	1799	1800
World's first parachute jump is made in France from a balloon	Department of the Navy is created		Washington D.C. officially becomes the nation's capital

Find the J. Adams stickers on sticker page A.

THOMAS JEFFERSON

3

President from 1801–1809

Thomas Jefferson never really thought of himself as a politician—but as a good citizen who wanted a country governed by the people. He was most proud of writing the Declaration of Independence and of starting the University of Virginia.

Martha "Patsy" Jefferson Randolph
Since Jefferson was a widower, his oldest daughter, Patsy, filled in as White House hostess. Her son was the first baby born in the White House.

A true believer in democracy, Jefferson had his dinner parties at a round table, and began the custom of shaking hands instead of bowing.

1743 - 1826

In 1806, explorers Lewis and Clark returned from their trip across the country with many gifts for the president—including a grizzly bear, which Jefferson kept in a cage on the White House lawn.

Ohio became a state. *Louisiana*, *Michigan*, and *Illinois* became territories.

In 1803, the U.S. nearly doubled its size when it purchased the Louisiana Territory from France for about three cents an acre.

Jefferson was a great inventor, and was also one of the first Americans to make macaroni and grow tomatoes (which many people thought were poisonous).

1801	1802	1803	1804	1805	1806	1807	1808	1809

First bananas are brought into the U.S.

Jefferson is reelected

Explorers Lewis and Clark reach the Pacific Ocean

First passenger steamship

Jefferson outlaws the African slave trade

5

Find the Jefferson stickers on sticker page A.

JAMES MADISON

Known as "the Father of the Constitution," James Madison helped write the Constitution and the Bill of Rights. But his good friend Thomas Jefferson had another nickname for the 5'4", 100-pound president—"the Great Little Madison."

Dolley Madison
Dolley Madison was preparing for a dinner party when the British invaded Washington. She fled with the Declaration of Independence and a portrait of George Washington. But the meal didn't go to waste—the British soldiers ate it!

Madison was the first president to serve ice cream at the White House!

1751 - 1836

Madison was the first president to wear long pants instead of knee breeches and stockings.

Louisiana and *Indiana* became states. *Missouri* and *Alabama* became territories.

During the War of 1812, the British set the White House and the Capitol on fire. Luckily, a summer thunderstorm put the fires out.

In 1814, Francis Scott Key wrote "The Star-Spangled Banner" as he watched the British bomb Fort McHenry.

1809	1810	1811	1812	1813	1814	1815	1816

First national road is built

War of 1812 begins
Madison is reelected

War of 1812 ends

First covered wagons take pioneers west

Find the Madison stickers on sticker page A.

5 JAMES MONROE

James Monroe's time as president was so popular, it was known as "the Era of Good Feelings." Monroe didn't even have to campaign for reelection. He is best remembered for his foreign policy; the Monroe Doctrine told European countries to stay out of North and South America.

Elizabeth Kortright Monroe
Elegant Elizabeth Monroe was called *la belle américaine*, or the beautiful American, by the French when Monroe was minister there.

1758 - 1831

President Monroe started his term with a four-month trip around the U.S.A.— while he waited for the White House to be repaired.

Monroe was the first president to ride in a steamboat.

Mississippi, Illinois, Alabama, Maine, and *Missouri* became states. *Arkansas* and *Florida* became territories.

In 1818, the first tin can in the U.S. was made.

In 1821, Troy Female Seminary, the first college for women in the U.S., opened.

Monroe moves into the restored White House

The U.S. buys Florida from Spain

Monroe is reelected

First public high school in the U.S. opens

Find the Monroe stickers on sticker page A.

JOHN QUINCY ADAMS

A great speaker and deal maker, John Quincy Adams was nick-named "Old Man Eloquent"—but in private he was pretty cold and grim. Adams stayed in politics even after he was president, serving in Congress until the day he died.

Louisa Johnson Adams
Louisa Adams was the only first lady born outside the U.S. She was born and raised in England.

1767 - 1848

John Quincy Adams was the first president to have his photograph taken.

Adams got his daily workout by skinny-dipping in the Potomac River every morning.

No new states were admitted.

In 1827, the first ballet in the U.S. was performed.

In 1828, Noah Webster published the first American dictionary.

1825	1826	1827	1828
Erie Canal opens	First photograph		First Native American newspaper

Find the J.Q. Adams stickers on sticker page A.

7 # ANDREW JACKSON

President from 1829–1837

Andrew Jackson was truly the first "People's President," and his campaign included picnics and barbecues all across the country. The War of 1812 had made Jackson a national hero—and earned the "tough-as-a-hickory-tree" general the nickname "Old Hickory."

Rachel Donelson Jackson
Andrew Jackson's beloved wife, Rachel, died right before he took office. She was buried in the same dress she'd bought for his inauguration.

Jackson was the first president born in a log cabin.

1767 - 1845

Arkansas and *Michigan* became states. *Wisconsin* became a territory.

Before he left the White House, Jackson had a huge open house party—complete with a 1,400-pound cheese. The smell of cheese stayed in the White House for weeks after he moved out.

In 1830, *Tom Thumb*, the first passenger steam locomotive in the U.S., was built—and Jackson became the first president to ride on a train.

In 1836, Texan fighters held off Mexican soldiers for two weeks at the famous battle of the Alamo.

1829	1830	1831	1832	1833	1834	1835	1836	1837

First American encyclopedia

Indian Removal Act gives the president the power to move eastern tribes west of the Mississippi

First oranges and lemons are brought to the U.S.

Andrew Jackson is reelected

First public library in the U.S.

First daily newspaper in the U.S.

Assassination attempt is made on Jackson's life (luckily, the gun does not fire)

White House gets running water

Texas Revolution begins

Find the Jackson stickers on sticker page A.

9

★8 MARTIN VAN BUREN

Martin Van Buren was the first president to be born a U.S. citizen. (Others had been born before the U.S. became a nation.) Although Van Buren wasn't born wealthy, he had a reputation for very expensive tastes.

Hannah Hoes Van Buren
Hannah, Van Buren's wife and childhood sweetheart, died nearly twenty years before he became president, and he never remarried.

Van Buren was nicknamed "Old Kinderhook" after the town where he was born—and some say it's where the expression "O.K." came from.

1782 - 1862

During Van Buren's term, thousands of banks and businesses closed, and millions of people lost everything they'd worked for.

Iowa became a territory.

In 1838, 14,000 Cherokee were forced to leave Georgia and march to Oklahoma. It became known as the Trail of Tears because so many people died along the way.

In 1839, the first baseball diamond was built in a cow pasture in Cooperstown, NY.

1837	1838	1839	1840
First steel plow / Queen Victoria is crowned Queen of England	White House gets hot water	Charles Goodyear patents rubber-making process	First photograph of the moon / Samuel Morse patents the telegraph

10

Find the Van Buren stickers on sticker page A.

WILLIAM HENRY HARRISON

President from March–April **1841**

William Henry Harrison's presidency was the shortest in history. He caught a cold on the same day he was sworn in and died of pneumonia just one month later. Like Washington and Jackson, he had been a famous war hero.

Anna Symmes Harrison
Anna Harrison was still living in Ohio and preparing to move to Washington when Harrison died. She is the only first lady to be the wife of one president and the grandmother of another—Benjamin Harrison.

To set himself apart from Van Buren and his fancy tastes, Harrison ran as "the Log Cabin Candidate"...even though he lived in a mansion.

1773 - 1841

Harrison liked to get up early and do his own shopping.

No new states were admitted.

Harrison was born on the Virginia plantation where the first Thanksgiving meal was held—two years before the famous Pilgrim dinner.

In 1841, Harrison delivered the longest inaugural address ever. In fact, his two-hour speech (which he gave outside in the cold) might have cost him his life.

 **1841**

Harrison is sworn in

Harrison becomes the first president to die in office

Find the W.H. Harrison stickers on sticker page A.

John Tyler was the first vice president to take over for a dead president. (And he hadn't even known President Harrison was sick!) Nicknaming him "His Accidency," Tyler's own party tried to take away much of his power. But Tyler refused...and soon became the first president without a political party.

Julia Gardiner Tyler
Tyler's first wife, Letitia, died a year after moving to the White House. In 1844, Tyler married Julia Gardiner—who started the tradition of having "Hail to the Chief" played for the president.

Years after he was president, during the Civil War, Tyler seceded with the South and became a congressman for the Confederate States of America. Because of this, until 1915, Tyler was officially a traitor.

1790 - 1862

Tyler had the most children of any president—fifteen! Tyler and his family were also animal lovers and always had lots of pets around.

Florida became a state.

In 1843, the 2,000-mile-long Oregon Trail opened for pioneers moving west.

In 1844, Samuel Morse sent the first telegraph message: "What hath God wrought."

1841	1842	1843	1844	1845
	First official baseball club / Letitia Tyler dies		Tyler marries Julia Gardiner	

Find the Tyler stickers on sticker page A.

★ 11 JAMES KNOX POLK

President from
1845–1849

James Polk sailed into office on the wave of "Manifest Destiny." This was the popular belief that the U.S. was meant to expand across all of North America. Hardworking Polk increased the size of the U.S. more than any president since Jefferson.

1795 - 1849

Sarah Childress Polk
Sarah Polk was one of the first first ladies to have a real say in her husband's work. She served as Polk's secretary and even helped him write speeches.

Polk was the first "dark horse"— or unexpected—candidate. He was so unknown that his opponent's slogan was "Who is Polk?"

James and Sarah Polk hosted the first formal Thanksgiving dinner ever served at the White House.

Texas, *Iowa*, and *Wisconsin* became states. *Oregon* and *Minnesota* became territories.

In 1847, the first U.S. postage stamps were made. Until then, people had just paid the postman.

In 1848, the first stick of chewing gum in the U.S. was sold.

1846	1847	1848	1849

Smithsonian Institution is founded

Mexican War begins

Gold is discovered in California

Mexican War ends

First women's rights convention is held in Seneca Falls, NY

Find the Polk stickers on sticker page A.

ZACHARY TAYLOR

12

Small and rather sloppy, General "Old Rough and Ready" Taylor was a Mexican War hero—not a politician. He'd never even voted in a presidential election!

Mary Elizabeth "Betty" Taylor Bliss
Because her mother, Margaret, did not want to be first lady, Taylor's daughter Betty served as White House hostess in her place. Mrs. Taylor chose to stay in her room and refused to pose for pictures.

By the time Taylor became president, the Underground Railroad was already helping thousands of slaves escape. Harriet Tubman was one of its leaders.

In 1849, the California Gold Rush began with 80,000 prospectors racing west.

1784 - 1850

Taylor brought his faithful warhorse, Old Whitey, to Washington with him and let him graze on the White House lawn—until sightseers started plucking Whitey's tail hairs!

No new states were admitted.

In 1850, Taylor took part in a hot Fourth of July ceremony at the unfinished Washington Monument, then went home to have some milk and cherries. Five days later, he died from a "digestive illness."

1849 **1850**

Safety pin is invented
Harriet Tubman escapes from slavery

Taylor dies

Find the Taylor stickers on sticker page A.

13 MILLARD FILLMORE

President from 1850–1853

The biggest question of Millard Fillmore's day was whether new states should allow slavery or not. The Northern states wanted to end it. The Southern ones wanted to keep it—and threatened to break away if they didn't get their way. Fillmore tried to compromise—it was called the Compromise of 1850.

Abigail Powers Fillmore
Twenty-one-year-old Abigail met nineteen-year-old Millard when he was her student in a one-room schoolhouse. Abigail was the first first lady to continue working after she was married.

Thanks to the Fillmores, the White House got many modern conveniences, including its first stove and tub.

In 1851, Amelia Bloomer shocked people by wearing lace pants under a short skirt—a style that was soon called "bloomers."

1800 - 1874

Mrs. Fillmore was so shocked to find the White House had no library, she asked the president to have Congress pay for one and picked out the books herself.

California became a state. *New Mexico*, *Utah*, and *Washington* became territories.

In 1852, Harriet Beecher Stowe published her antislavery novel, *Uncle Tom's Cabin*.

1850   1851   1852   1853

Compromise of 1850 outlaws slavery in CA, but allows Southern slave owners to capture slaves who escape North

Isaac Singer patents his sewing machine

First successful airship is flown

Find the Fillmore stickers on sticker page B.

FRANKLIN PIERCE

President from 1853–1857

Handsome Franklin Pierce never, ever lost an election. He hoped to calm down the North and South by letting new states decide for themselves whether to allow slavery, but this only started more fighting for control.

Jane Appleton Pierce
For two years after her eleven-year-old son was killed in a train accident, Jane Pierce refused to appear in public. He was, in fact, their third son to die.

Another "dark horse" candidate, Pierce ran on the slogan "We *Polked* you in 1844. We'll *Pierce* you in 1852."

1804 - 1869

In 1854, the first U.S. oil company—Pennsylvania Rock Oil—was formed.

Pierce was known to race his horse and carriage through the streets of Washington—and was once even arrested for knocking over an old woman.

Kansas and *Nebraska* became territories.

In 1856, the first U.S. kindergarten opened.

1853	1854	1855	1856
The U.S. buys parts of Arizona and New Mexico from Mexico	Kansas-Nebraska Act is passed, allowing states to choose whether to allow slavery	Republican Party is formed	

Find the Pierce stickers on sticker page B.

JAMES BUCHANAN

15

James Buchanan had the unusual problem of being nearsighted in one eye and farsighted in the other—but he still managed to have the neatest handwriting of any president.

Harriet Lane
Buchanan was the only president who never married. His niece, Harriet Lane, served as his White House hostess.

1791 - 1868

Because Buchanan had been working in England, he was able to avoid the subject of slavery in his campaign—and easily beat the new Republican, antislavery party.

In 1860, Pony Express service began carrying mail across the West.

Buchanan was the first president to have a royal guest stay in the White House—England's Prince Albert. Buchanan even slept on the sofa so the prince could use his bed.

Minnesota, *Oregon*, and *Kansas* became states. *Colorado*, *Nevada*, and the *Dakotas* became territories.

In 1861, seven Southern states broke away from the Union and formed the Confederate States of America.

1857	1858	1859	1860	1861

First passenger elevator

Panic of 1857 puts millions out of work

Darwin publishes his theory of evolution

South Carolina secedes from the Union

Find the Buchanan stickers on sticker page B.

ABRAHAM LINCOLN

President from 1861–1865

Abraham Lincoln was one of America's greatest leaders. If it weren't for him, we might be two separate nations today! Still, Lincoln never lost his knack for telling jokes and stories—or his pioneer accent. He was the first president born west of the original thirteen states.

Mary Todd Lincoln
Mary Lincoln's White House years were far from happy. Besides the great war, she had to face the deaths of her son Willie and her husband.

One month after Lincoln was sworn in, the new Confederate army began firing on Fort Sumter, officially beginning the Civil War.

In 1863, Lincoln issued the Emancipation Proclamation, freeing slaves in the Confederate States—but not in the Union.

1809 - 1865

Lincoln was the first president to wear a beard in office—which he grew at the suggestion of an eleven-year-old girl. He was also the first president to have his picture on a coin.

West Virginia and *Nevada* became states. *Arizona*, *Idaho*, and *Montana* became territories.

On April 14, 1865, just five days after the South surrendered, John Wilkes Booth snuck into the president's box at Ford's Theater and shot Lincoln in the back of the head.

1861	1862	1863	1864	1865
Civil War begins / U.S. issues its first paper money	Lincoln's son Willie dies	First roller skates / Lincoln makes Thanksgiving a national holiday	Lincoln is reelected	General Robert E. Lee surrenders and the Civil War ends / Lincoln is assassinated

Find the Lincoln stickers on sticker page B.

17 ANDREW JOHNSON

Andrew Johnson never went to school and had to teach himself to read. Like Lincoln, he wanted to bring the North and South back together. Many congressmen did not agree with this approach and tried unsuccessfully to remove Johnson from office through an impeachment trial.

Eliza McCardle Johnson
Married when she was just sixteen, Eliza Johnson taught her young husband writing and math.

1808 - 1875

Johnson was trained as a tailor and opened his own shop when he was just seventeen. As president, he sometimes still sewed his own clothes.

Nebraska became a state. *Wyoming* became a territory.

In 1866, the first U.S. Civil Rights Act was passed. The Act gave Americans of every race equal rights under the law.

In 1866, Alfred Nobel of Sweden invented dynamite.

In 1867, Secretary of State William Seward bought Alaska from Russia for about 2 cents an acre. Critics called it "Seward's Folly"—until gold was found there. Then it was called the biggest bargain in history.

1865	1866	1867	1868	1869

First train robbery

13th Amendment outlaws slavery

Civil Rights Act of 1866 is passed

American Society for the Prevention of Cruelty to Animals (ASPCA) is founded

First typewriter

House impeaches Johnson, but the Senate acquits him

14th Amendment makes former slaves citizens and gives them full civil rights

Find the A. Johnson stickers on sticker page B.

18 ULYSSES S. GRANT

As the general who led the Union armies to victory, Ulysses S. Grant was a presidential shoo-in. Grant was actually born Hiram Ulysses Grant. But when his name was put down as Ulysses Simpson Grant by mistake on his West Point application, Grant liked the initials U.S.G. so much better than H.U.G., he decided to keep them.

Julia Dent Grant
Julia Grant's White House years were the happiest of her life—and if it had been up to "Mrs. G.," as Grant called her, he would have run for a third term.

1822 - 1885

"Let Us Have Peace" became the theme of Grant's campaign—and is even engraved on his tomb in New York City.

As president, Grant once was given a speeding ticket for riding too fast through the streets of Washington.

Colorado became a state.

In 1869, the first cross-country railroad in the U.S. was completed and marked by a golden spike.

In 1872, Grant named the first national park—Yellowstone, home of Old Faithful.

1869	1870	1871	1872	1873	1874	1875	1876
Susan B. Anthony and Elizabeth Cady Stanton form the National Woman Suffrage Association	Brooklyn Bridge is begun	P.T. Barnum opens "the Greatest Show on Earth" / Great Chicago fire destroys much of the city	Victoria Woodhull becomes the first woman to run for president / Grant is reelected		First zoo in the U.S.	Alexander Graham Bell invents the telephone	Sioux and Cheyenne warriors defeat Gen. Custer at the battle of Little Bighorn

Find the Grant stickers on sticker page B.

RUTHERFORD B. HAYES

President from 1877–1881

Rutherford Birchard Hayes was an honest, religious man, who began his days with a prayer and ended them with a hymn. Still, his election was the most disputed ever. It took Congress months to decide which candidate had the most electoral votes. In the end, Hayes won by only one, and was called by many "His Fraudulency."

Lucy Webb Hayes
Lucy Hayes was the first first lady with a college degree, and the first to be called "first lady." She was also known as "Lemonade Lucy" because she never served alcohol in the White House.

In 1877, Thomas Edison went to the White House to show his new phonograph to the president.

1822 - 1893

Hayes was the first president to have a telephone and a typewriter in the White House.

No new states were admitted.

 In 1878, the Hayeses hosted the first official Easter Egg Roll on the White House lawn—which is still held every year.

 In 1880, the first hot dog was served in St. Louis, Missouri.

1877	1878	1879	1880	1881

Reconstruction ends

Thomas Edison invents the light bulb

Hayes becomes the first president to visit the west coast

Metropolitan Museum of Art opens in New York City

Find the Hayes stickers on sticker page B.

Four months after he was sworn in, James Abram Garfield was shot as he walked through a train station. He died from blood poisoning ten weeks later. The killer had hoped to get a job from the new president, and was angry because he never did.

Lucretia Rudolph Garfield
Lucretia "Crete" Garfield was recovering from an illness at the New Jersey shore when she heard that her husband had been shot, but she returned to Washington right away and helped nurse him until he died.

Garfield did most of his campaigning from his front porch in Ohio—where people came by train to hear him speak.

In 1881, the first malted milk was served. Yum!

1831 - 1881

Garfield was the first left-handed president. He liked to show off by writing Greek with one hand and Latin with the other—at the same time!

No new states were admitted.

Also in 1881, nurse Clara Barton founded the American Red Cross.

1881

First summer camp in the U.S.

Garfield is shot by Charles Guiteau

Garfield dies

Find the Garfield stickers on sticker page B.

CHESTER A. ARTHUR

President from 1881–1885

Tall, handsome Chester Alan Arthur liked fancy clothes so much, he had eighty pairs of pants! He liked fine furniture, too, and had the White House redecorated from top to bottom in the latest fashion.

Ellen Herndon Arthur
Ellen "Nell" Arthur died just a year before her husband became president. From then on, Arthur placed flowers by her picture every day.

1829 - 1886

Arthur shook so many hands when he campaigned, his hand swelled up and his ring had to be filed off.

Arthur liked to stay up very late, and hardly ever went to bed before two a.m. One of his favorite things to do was give guests tours of Washington in the middle of the night.

No new states were admitted.

In 1885, the world's first skyscraper was built—the ten-story Home Insurance Building in Chicago.

In 1883, Buffalo Bill Cody put on his first Wild West Show.

1881 **1882** **1883** **1884** **1885**

Shoot-out at the O.K. Corral

Brooklyn Bridge opens

Washington Monument is dedicated

23

Find the Arthur stickers on sticker page B.

Grover Cleveland was actually born Stephen Grover Cleveland, but he dropped his first name when he was a young man. Cleveland was so large and jolly, his nieces and nephews called him Uncle Jumbo.

Frances Folsom Cleveland
Twenty-one-year-old Frances Cleveland was the youngest first lady ever—and one of the most popular.

A "do-it-yourself" kind of president, Cleveland even went without a secretary for a while and answered the White House phone himself.

In 1886, John Pemberton invented Coca-Cola as a health tonic.

1837-1908

Cleveland was the only president to get married in the White House.

No new states were admitted.

Also in 1886, Cleveland dedicated the Statue of Liberty in New York City.

1885	1886	1887	1888	1889
	Cleveland marries Frances Folsom		Kodak box camera is introduced — National Geographic Society is founded	

Find the Cleveland stickers on sticker page B.

★ 23 BENJAMIN HARRISON

President from 1889-1893

The grandson of President William Henry Harrison, Benjamin Harrison was the last president to wear a beard, and was so stiff and formal, people often called him "the human iceberg."

Caroline Scott Harrison
Caroline Harrison put up the first White House Christmas tree. Sadly, she died in the White House just two weeks before the 1892 election.

Nicknamed "Little Ben" because he was just 5'6" tall, Harrison told voters not to worry—"Grandfather's Hat Fits."

In 1891, basketball was invented by a gym teacher named James Naismith.

1833 - 1901

Harrison was the first president to have electricity in the White House—but his wife and he were so afraid to touch the switches, they left the lights on all night long.

North Dakota, South Dakota, Montana, Washington, Idaho, and Wyoming became states. Oklahoma became a territory.

In 1892, Ellis Island opened to receive new immigrants pouring into New York.

1889	**1890**	**1891**	**1892**	**1893**
White settlers claim 2 million acres of former Indian land in Oklahoma in one day / First movie camera	Sitting Bull is killed		Caroline Harrison dies / First gas-powered car in the U.S.	

25

Find the B. Harrison stickers on sticker page B.

★ 24 GROVER CLEVELAND

Grover Cleveland was the only president to be reelected after being voted out of office. And his second daughter, Esther, was the first child of a president to be born in the White House.

Frances Folsom Cleveland
At the end of Cleveland's first term, Frances Cleveland had told the White House servants she wanted "everything just the way it is now when we come back." Obviously, she knew what she was saying!

In 1893, Cleveland had a tumor secretly removed from his mouth—and the operation stayed a secret until years after his death.

In 1893, the world's biggest Ferris wheel (it was 25 stories tall!) was built for the Chicago World's Columbian Exposition.

1837 - 1908

The Baby Ruth candy bar was named after Cleveland's baby daughter Ruth.

Utah became a state.

In 1896, the first modern Olympic Games were held in Athens, Greece.

1893	1894	1895	1896	1897

Panic of 1893 starts economic depression

First zipper

Canada introduces ice hockey to the U.S.

Cleveland makes Labor Day a national holiday

Dr. John Harvey Kellogg invents cornflakes

First professional football game

First radio

First comic strip

Henry Ford builds his first car

First campaign buttons

Find the Cleveland stickers on sticker page B.

WILLIAM McKINLEY

President from 1897-1901

It was during William McKinley's term that the U.S. became a true "world power." The Spanish-American War was won in just 100 days—then the U.S. acquired Puerto Rico, the Philippines, Guam, and Hawaii.

Ida Saxton McKinley
President McKinley was completely devoted to his wife, Ida—who suffered from what people then called "the falling sickness." Today we call it epilepsy.

1843 - 1901

McKinley never campaigned without a lucky red carnation in his buttonhole. His home state, Ohio, later made it their state flower.

After the sinking of the battleship *Maine* in 1898, "Remember the *Maine*!" became the battle cry of the Spanish-American War.

McKinley was the first president to ride to his inauguration in a car—and the only one to have a parrot who could whistle "Yankee Doodle."

Hawaii became a territory.

 McKinley was assassinated just six months into his second term. After that, Congress gave the Secret Service the job of protecting the president full-time.

1897 — First U.S. subway opens in Boston

1898 — Spanish-American War

1899

1900 — McKinley is reelected

1901 — Oil is discovered in Texas

McKinley is shot by anarchist Leon Czolgosz as he shakes hands in a receiving line; he dies eight days later

Find the McKinley stickers on sticker page C.

26 THEODORE ROOSEVELT

President from 1901–1909

Theodore Roosevelt was the youngest president, taking over for McKinley when he was only 42. Roosevelt worked to make the U.S. stronger abroad and at home, where he believed every American deserved a "square deal"—fair wages, fair prices, and safe, healthy conditions.

Edith Carow Roosevelt
Edith Roosevelt grew up next door to the future president (and her future husband). They were playmates, but they did not get married until after the death of Roosevelt's first wife.

Teddy Roosevelt was a sickly boy, but he grew up to be one of our most athletic presidents. He liked to hunt, climb mountains, and practice boxing and judo.

1858 - 1919

Roosevelt was the first president to ride in an airplane and a submarine.

Oklahoma became a state.

In 1902, a toymaker saw a cartoon showing T.R. on a hunting trip saying "No" to shooting a little bear cub. The toymaker named one of his stuffed bears "Teddy's bear" and put it in the window—and the teddy bear was born!

Nicknamed "the Great Conservationist," Roosevelt established hundreds of national forests and parks.

1901 1902 1903 1904 1905 1906 1907 1908

- First World Series
- Wright brothers' first airplane flight
- First reported UFO sighting
- Work begins on the Panama Canal
- First ice-cream cone and first hamburger
- Roosevelt is reelected
- Einstein publishes his theory of relativity
- Roosevelt is the first president to win the Nobel Peace Prize
- Great San Francisco earthquake and fire
- First radio broadcast
- Ford's Model T goes on sale
- First Mother's Day celebration

Find the T. Roosevelt stickers on sticker page C.

27 WILLIAM H. TAFT

President from 1909–1913

William Howard Taft loved the law—but he did not love being president. His favorite job came later, when President Harding made him Chief Justice of the Supreme Court. Taft is the only man to have done both jobs.

Helen "Nellie" Taft
Before she even moved into the White House, Nellie Taft ordered the first presidential automobiles and had the old White House stables turned into a garage.

Before he left office, Theodore Roosevelt hand-picked Taft to be his successor. The public soon nicknamed him Bill—but his good friends called him Will.

1857 - 1930

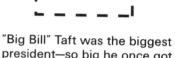

"Big Bill" Taft was the biggest president—so big he once got stuck in the White House tub. After that, he had a new tub put in—big enough to hold four men!

Arizona and *New Mexico* became states. *Alaska* became a territory.

Taft was a big baseball fan, and was the first president to throw out the first ball on opening day.

In 1911, the first comic book was published.

1909   **1910**   **1911**   **1912**   **1913**

First cartoon
National Association for the Advancement of Colored People (NAACP) is founded
North Pole is discovered
Boy Scouts of America is founded
First Father's Day
Oreo cookie is invented
South Pole is discovered
First Indianapolis 500 car race
Girl Scouts of the U.S.A. is founded
The *Titanic* sinks

Find the Taft stickers on sticker page C.

WOODROW WILSON

Woodrow Wilson was one of the most scholarly presidents, earning over a dozen degrees. He led the U.S. to victory in World War I, but more than anything he wanted world peace. Wilson's idea for a "League of Nations" led to the formation of today's United Nations.

Edith Bolling Wilson
It's said that Edith Wilson was directly descended from Pocahontas. She married the president in 1915, one year after his first wife died. After Wilson had a stroke in 1919, she helped him with many of his presidential duties.

At first, Wilson promised to keep the U.S. out of WWI. But by 1917, it was clear that in order to make the world "safe for democracy," the U.S. would have to join in.

World War I ended in 1918, after four long years and the loss of 10 million soldiers. It was supposed to be "the war to end all wars."

1856 - 1924

During WWI, Wilson kept sheep on the White House lawn. Their wool was used to make army blankets—and the lawn never had to be mowed.

Puerto Rico became a territory.

 In 1920, the 14th Amendment gave women the right to vote.

1913	1914	1915	1916	1917	1918	1919	1920
	Panama Canal opens / World War I begins	First U.S. taxicabs	Wilson is reelected	Russian Revolution / U.S. joins in WWI / Prohibition outlaws liquor	First airmail delivery / World War I ends	Wilson's stroke	League of Nations is formed—but Congress votes not to join / Wilson receives Nobel Peace Prize

Find the Wilson stickers on sticker page C.

WARREN G. HARDING

President from 1921–1923

Warren Gamaliel Harding loved poker—and even lost President Benjamin Harrison's White House china in a game! There were many scandals in Harding's administration—but they were not exposed until after his sudden death on a goodwill trip across the country.

Florence Kling Harding
"The Duchess," as President Harding called his wife, Florence, liked to edit her husband's speeches. She also liked to lead White House tours.

1865 - 1923

Harding promised the country a "return to normalcy" after World War I. He was the first president that women could vote for.

In 1921, the first Miss America pageant was held.

Every day, Harding's dog Laddie Boy would bring him the morning paper. After the president died, paperboys around the country collected pennies to build a statue of Laddie Boy—which is now on display at the Smithsonian Institution.

No new states were admitted.

In 1922, Harding gave the first presidential speech over the radio.

1921
First Band-Aids

1922
Lincoln Memorial is dedicated
Soviet Union is formed
First water skis

1923
Harding dies suddenly of a mysterious illness (doctors believe it was a heart attack)

Find the Harding stickers on sticker page C.

CALVIN COOLIDGE

President from 1923-1929

"Silent Cal" Coolidge was a man of few words and few smiles—but he governed during the oh-so-carefree "Roaring Twenties." When President Harding died, V.P. Coolidge was visiting his family in Vermont. So his father, a justice of the peace, got to swear in Coolidge in the very house where he was born.

Grace Goodhue Coolidge
Grace Coolidge was just about the most popular American woman of her day. Before she was married, she taught lipreading to the deaf, and as first lady once gave a speech entirely in sign language.

Coolidge believed the less government the better, and in many ways let the country run itself. Coolidge also got more sleep than any other president—around eleven hours a day.

1872 - 1933

Coolidge got his exercise riding a mechanical horse he had installed in his White House bedroom.

No new states were admitted.

In 1927, Charles Lindbergh made the first nonstop solo flight across the Atlantic.

The Coolidges loved animals and got all kinds of pets as gifts, but their favorite was a raccoon they named Rebecca—who had actually been given to them as an exotic Thanksgiving main dish!

1923	1924	1925	1926	1927	1928	1929
	Native Americans are made "official" U.S. citizens / Coolidge wins election	John Scopes is convicted for teaching evolution in school	First rocket flight / First talking movie	Babe Ruth sets home run record / First TV	Mickey Mouse debuts	First vending machine

Find the Coolidge stickers on sticker page C.

★ 31 HERBERT HOOVER

President from 1929–1933

Until Herbert Clark Hoover (or "Bert," as his friends called him) ran for president, he had never run for office. He was a self-made millionaire devoted to helping people. But he also led the U.S. through one of its worst economic times.

Lou Henry Hoover
Lou and Herbert Hoover met at Stanford University, where she was the first woman to get a geology degree. She and Hoover spoke several languages, including Chinese, which they used when they didn't want others to know what they were saying.

Hoover's campaign promise to put "a chicken in every pot—and a car in every garage" was one which he couldn't keep.

1874 - 1964

During the Great Depression, Hoover's name became a dirty word. Shantytowns were called "Hoovervilles." Newspapers were "Hoover blankets." And the wild rabbits and squirrels people killed for food were called "Hoover hogs."

No new states were admitted.

In 1929, the same year Hoover took office, the stock market crashed, and the Great Depression began.

In 1931, the Empire State Building was opened—and was the tallest buiding in the world for nearly forty years.

1929	1930	1931	1932	1933
First Academy Awards	First pinball machine	"The Star-Spangled Banner" becomes the national anthem / First air conditioner	Amelia Earhart flies solo across the Atlantic	

Find the Hoover stickers on sticker page C.

Franklin Delano Roosevelt led the U.S. out of the Great Depression and to victory in World War II. And he did it all from a wheelchair—since polio had left him paralyzed at the age of 39.

Anna Eleanor Roosevelt
Little did Eleanor Roosevelt know when her uncle, President Teddy Roosevelt, gave her away that she was marrying a future president too. After FDR lost use of his legs, she traveled around the world as his eyes and ears.

FDR was elected four times—more than any other president. Later, in 1951, Congress passed the 22nd Amendment, limiting the president to just two terms.

In 1933, the chocolate chip cookie was invented.

1882 - 1945

FDR's Scottie, Fala, got the nickname "the Informer" from the Secret Service—who knew that whenever they saw Fala, the president couldn't be far away.

No new states were admitted.

FDR had hoped to keep the U.S. out of WWII. But by 1941, he knew the U.S. had to join in too. Sadly, he died just months before Germany and Japan surrendered.

1933
- Adolph Hitler becomes leader of Germany
- Prohibition ends
- First drive-in movie

1935
- Nylon is invented
- First Heisman Trophy

1937
- First helicopter flight
- FDR is reelected
- Amelia Earhart disappears

1939
- First ballpoint pen
- Great Britain and France declare war on Germany

1941
- First McDonald's
- FDR is reelected
- Mount Rushmore is finished
- Japan attacks Pearl Harbor and the U.S. declares war

1943
- U.S. tests first jet

1945
- D-Day
- FDR is reelected
- FDR dies

Find the F.D. Roosevelt stickers on sticker page C.

33 HARRY S TRUMAN

By the time he was fourteen, Harry S Truman had read every book in his town's library. But what did the "S" in his name stand for, you ask? Not a thing. Because his parents couldn't decide which grandfather to name him after (Shippe or Solomon) they left his middle name just plain "S."

Elizabeth "Bess" Truman
Bess and Harry Truman went to the same school from the fifth grade on. At the White House, Bess, Harry, and their daughter Margaret were together so much, the staff called them "The Three Musketeers."

1884 - 1972

In 1945, Truman made the decision to drop two atomic bombs on Japan. One day later, Japan surrendered and World War II was over.

No new states were admitted.

Truman was so far behind in the polls in 1948 that one paper went ahead and printed that his opponent had won. Boy, were they surprised when Truman came out ahead!

In 1946, the first computer, ENIAC, was introduced. No laptop—this thing weighed thirty tons!

In 1952, Truman gave the first televised tour of the White House.

1945	1946	1947	1948	1949	1950	1951	1952	1953

World War II ends
The United Nations is formed

Jackie Robinson becomes the first black major league baseball player

First Polaroid camera

Truman orders desegregation of U.S. Armed Forces

"Cold War" officially begins
Truman is elected

First nonstop round-the-world flight

Korean War begins

First color TV show

35

Find the Truman stickers on sticker page C.

★ 34 DWIGHT D. EISENHOWER

President from **1953–1961**

As the Supreme Commander of the victorious armies in Europe, General Dwight David ("Ike") Eisenhower was so popular after World War II that *both* political parties asked him to run for president!

Mamie Doud Eisenhower
As an army officer's wife, Mamie Eisenhower moved 27 times in 37 years. Her eight years in the White House were the most she'd spent in one place since her marriage.

What did Ike like? Golf was his favorite sport, but he also liked to paint, and set up an art studio in the White House.

1890 - 1969

In 1954, the Supreme Court ruled that black and white children could no longer be forced to go to separate schools.

Alaska and *Hawaii* became states—and there were fifty!

In 1955, Disneyland opened.

In 1957, the Soviet Union got a head start on the space race by shooting the satellite *Sputnik* into orbit

1953	1954	1955	1956	1957	1958	1959	1960
First 3-D movie / Korean War ends	First atomic power plant / Elvis Presley records his first song	First televised presidential news conference / Rosa Parks, a black woman, is arrested for not giving up her bus seat in a "whites only" section	Eisenhower is reelected	Eisenhower sends troops to make sure a public school in Arkansas admits black students	First American space satellite launched	First 7 U.S. astronauts are picked	First aluminum cans

Find the Eisenhower stickers on sticker page C.

JOHN F. KENNEDY

President from 1961–1963

At 43, John Fitzgerald Kennedy was the youngest president ever elected—and the youngest to die. His assassination shocked the country and is still a mystery—since the suspect, Lee Harvey Oswald, was killed before he could go to trial.

Jacqueline Bouvier Kennedy
Jackie Kennedy worked to make the White House into a historic and cultural showplace. Of course, she's probably best remembered for her stylish "Jackie look," which women around the world tried to copy.

JFK declared that the torch of government had passed to a "new generation of Americans," and urged young people to "Ask not what your country can do for you—ask what you can do for your country."

1917 - 1963

Kennedy was the first Boy Scout to become president.

No new states were admitted.

Also in 1961, Alan Shepard became the first American to go into space—three weeks after the Soviet Union's first man.

In 1961, in Germany, Communist East Berlin and free West Berlin were officially divided by the Berlin Wall.

1961   1962   1963

Peace Corps is founded

U.S. sends first chimpanzee into space

John Glenn becomes the first American to orbit the earth

Martin Luther King, Jr., leads Freedom March to Washington D.C.

JFK is assassinated

Find the Kennedy stickers on sticker page C.

LYNDON B. JOHNSON

President from 1963–1969

Lyndon Baines Johnson wanted to build a "Great Society" for all Americans, regardless of their color or how much money they made. But his years in office saw a divided society instead...divided over the Vietnam War...divided over civil rights...and, of course, divided between "hippies" and the "establishment."

Claudia "Lady Bird" Johnson
A nurse gave Lady Bird Johnson her nickname on the day she was born, when she told her parents that she was "as purty as a ladybird." Johnson proposed to her on their very first date.

"LBJ" weren't just Johnson's initials—they were also the initials of his wife and daughters (Lynda Bird and Luci Baines), his Texas ranch, and his dogs, Little Beagle Johnson and Little Beagle Junior.

1908 - 1973

LBJ liked to give guests to his ranch ninety mile-per-hour tours in his favorite Lincoln Continental.

No new states were admitted.

In 1967, the Green Bay Packers beat the Kansas City Chiefs in the very first Super Bowl.

By 1968, the Vietnam War had made Johnson so unpopular, he announced that he would not run for reelection.

1963	1964	1965	1966	1967	1968
Two days after JFK's assassination, Jack Ruby shoots suspect Lee Harvey Oswald	The Beatles "invade" the U.S. / Congress gives LBJ power to use military force in Vietnam	LBJ is elected / First space walk / Civil rights riots in Los Angeles / First miniskirt	National Organization of Women is founded	First human heart transplant / LBJ appoints the first black Supreme Court justice—Thurgood Marshall	Martin Luther King, Jr., is assassinated / First U.S. astronauts orbit the moon

Find the L.B. Johnson stickers on sticker page C.

RICHARD M. NIXON

President from 1969–1974

Richard Milhous Nixon was the first president to visit all fifty states, and the only one to resign from office. If he hadn't stepped down, he might have been the first president to be impeached for his part in the scandalous Watergate break-in.

Patricia Ryan Nixon
Pat Nixon met her husband at tryouts for a play at a local theater. Not only did they each get the part—but Nixon proposed to her that very day.

Nixon played a mean game of poker—and it's said he won enough while he was in the Navy to pay for his first political campaign.

In 1969, Neil Armstrong and Edwin Aldrin became the first men to walk on the moon.

1913 - 1994

In 1972, five men were arrested for breaking into Democratic party headquarters in the Watergate Hotel in Washington D.C. At first Nixon said he knew nothing about it. But audiotapes later showed that he had.

No new states were admitted.

Also in 1969, the original Woodstock music festival was held.

1969	1970	1971	1972	1973	1974
Sesame Street debuts	First Earth Day / World Trade Center is built	26th Amendment lowers the voting age from 21 to 18 / Nixon becomes the first president to visit China and Moscow	Last U.S. combat troops leave Vietnam / Nixon is reelected in a landslide victory	Sears Tower is built / Vice President Spiro Agnew resigns after he is charged with taking bribes / Gerald Ford is named the new vice president	Little League is opened to girls / Congress begins Nixon impeachment hearings / Nixon resigns

Find the Nixon stickers on sticker page D.

GERALD R. FORD

Gerald Rudolph Ford got to be president in a most unusual way: First he was appointed by President Nixon to replace Vice President Agnew, who had been forced to resign. Then, when Nixon was himself forced to resign, Vice President Ford suddenly became President Ford!

Elizabeth "Betty" Ford
A former dancer and model, Betty Ford was a very popular first lady who actively supported women's rights. She's also known for the Betty Ford Clinic for alcohol and drug dependency, which she founded after she left the White House.

Ford was a football star in college, and was even offered contracts by professional teams. Instead, he went to Yale Law School, where he made extra money as the football coach and as a model.

1913 - 2006

In 1976, the U.S. celebrated its Bicentennial—the 200th birthday of the Declaration of Independence!

No new states were admitted.

In 1976, *Viking 1* became the first U.S. spacecraft to land on Mars.

Ford's daughter, Susan, had her senior prom in the White House.

1974   1975   1976

Vietnam War officially ends

U.S. and Soviet ships link in space

Two failed assassination attempts are made on Ford's life

First VCR

40

Find the Ford stickers on sticker page D.

JIMMY CARTER

Jimmy Carter tried to make the White House a more informal, comfortable place. He did away with trumpet fanfares, carried his own bags, and built his daughter, Amy, a tree house on the White House Lawn.

Rosalynn Smith Carter
Both Rosalynn and Jimmy Carter tried to set good examples for the American people. During the energy crisis, they kept the heat so low in the winter, Rosalynn had to wear long underwear around the White House.

Before getting into politics, Carter ran his family's peanut farm in Georgia. His very first job was selling boiled peanuts on the streets when he was five.

1924 -

Carter was the first president born in a hospital.

No new states were admitted.

In 1980, Mount St. Helens in Washington State erupted. It was the first volcano to blow up in the U.S. since 1921.

In 1978, Carter helped negotiate the historic Camp David Peace Accord between longtime enemies Egypt and Israel.

1977	1978	1979	1980	1981

- First personal computer
- First test tube baby
- First transatlantic balloon crossing
- First Walkman
- Three Mile Island nuclear power plant accident
- Over 60 Americans are taken hostage at the U.S. embassy in Iran
- First Rollerblades
- U.S. boycotts Summer Olympics in Moscow to protest Soviet invasion of Afghanistan
- Mission to rescue hostages in Iran fails

Find the Carter stickers on sticker page D.

☆ 40 RONALD REAGAN

A former actor, Ronald Reagan was so good at using television to get his ideas across to the people, he earned the nickname "the Great Communicator." He was also the first president to wear contact lenses.

Nancy Davis Reagan
Ronald and Nancy Reagan met in Hollywood, where she was acting in movies too. They made only one movie together—*Hellcats of the Navy*.

Reagan liked to keep a jar of his favorite food—jelly beans—on his desk. He also liked to read newspapers from around the country every morning—comics first!

In 1981, the space shuttle made its first flight—and became the world's first reusable spacecraft.

1911 - 2004

Reagan was the only professional actor to become president. He made 53 movies before he moved on to politics.

No new states were admitted.

In 1983, the first CD players were sold.

1981	1982	1983	1984	1985	1986	1987	1988
Hostages in Iran are released	MTV debuts	First artificial heart implant	Reagan is reelected	The *Titanic* is found	The space shuttle *Challenger* explodes	First snowboard	U.S. and U.S.S.R. agree to reduce nuclear weapons
John Hinckley, Jr., shoots and wounds Reagan and three others	Reagan appoints the first female Supreme Court justice—Sandra Day O'Connor				Iran-Contra scandal is exposed		

Find the Reagan stickers on sticker page D.

President from 1989–1993

George Bush was the first sitting vice president since Martin Van Buren to run for and win the presidency. And he was only the second president to have a son who also became president.

Barbara Pierce Bush
Barbara Bush might be the only first lady to have a World War II bomber named after her. When George was a pilot in the Navy, he named his airplane in her honor.

1924 -

"Read my lips: No new taxes!" was Bush's motto during his campaign—but it was "Read my lips: No more broccoli!" after the election. Bush hated broccoli so much, he had it banned from all White House menus.

In 1990, the Bushes' springer spaniel Millie "wrote" a best-selling book (with a little help from Mrs. Bush).

No new states were admitted.

In 1990, East and West Germany were reunited, the Berlin Wall was broken down—and Bush soon declared the Cold War over.

In 1991, the U.S. declared war on Iraq. Six weeks later, Iraq surrendered and Desert Storm, as the war was called, was over.

1989	1990	1991	1992	1993

Exxon *Valdez* spills 10 million barrels of oil off the Alaskan coast

First laptop computer

500th anniversary of Columbus's voyage to America

Find the Bush stickers on sticker page D.

BILL CLINTON

William Jefferson Clinton was the first president to be born after World War II. Because of personal scandals, this popular president was the second president to be impeached by the House of Representatives. However, the Senate decided that he should not be removed from office.

Hillary Rodham Clinton
Hillary Clinton stopped practicing law when she moved to the White House. In 2000, she became the first First Lady to be elected to the U.S. Senate.

1946 -

Clinton was the only president to play the saxophone on TV. And in high school, he played in a jazz band called the Three Blind Mice.

No new states were admitted.

Clinton and Vice President Al Gore were the first running mates to campaign across the country in a bus.

In 1994, Clinton started Americorps—a national service program especially for young people.

In 1995, the Million Man March drew African American men from across the country to Washington D.C.

1993	1994	1995	1996	1997	1998	1999	2000
World Trade Center is bombed; Whitewater investment scandal is exposed	Woodstock II music festival; Leaders of Israel, Palestine, and Jordan sign peace agreements; Baseball strike begins	Baseball strike ends; Federal Building in Oklahoma City is bombed	Clinton is reelected		At age 77, John Glenn, who orbited the earth in 1962, flies another U.S. space mission; The House impeaches President Clinton	Michael Jordan retires from the Chicago Bulls	Vladimir Putin is elected President of Russia, succeeding Boris Yeltsin

Find the Clinton stickers on sticker page D.

43 GEORGE W. BUSH

2001–2009

George W. Bush is only the second president to have a father who has also served as president. The second President Bush says that as a kid he dreamed about being a professional baseball player. In one of the closest elections in the history of the United States, it took many weeks to confirm that Mr. Bush was the winner.

Laura Welch Bush
Laura Bush grew up in Midland, Texas, where friends introduced her to George W. Bush in 1977. They were married just three months later. Laura Bush was a public school teacher with a master's degree in library science.

1946 -

George W. Bush was the first president to be elected in the twenty-first century.

No new states were admitted.

Thanks to the Internet, millions of people around the world can communicate daily with each other!

George W. Bush and a group of investors once owned the Texas Rangers baseball franchise.

2001	2003	2004	2005	2007
Attacks on the World Trade Center and the Pentagon	The U.S. invades Iraq to search for weapons of mass destruction, marking the beginning of the Iraq War	Bush is reelected despite controversy about the Iraq War · Boston Red Sox win the World Series for the first time since 1918	Hurricane Katrina destroys land across the Mississippi coast, including the city of New Orleans	Barry Bonds breaks Hank Aaron's home run record

Find the G.W. Bush stickers on page D.

WHO WILL BE THE NEXT

JOHN McCAIN

John McCain is the Republican candidate. He is a senator from Arizona. Senator McCain attended the United States Naval Academy and fought in the Vietnam War as a naval aviator, flying attack planes from the decks of ships. Senator McCain tried to become the candidate in 2000. But he lost the Republican nomination to George W. Bush in a tight race. If Senator McCain wins the election in 2008, he will be the oldest person, at age 72, to ever be voted into the White House. That's older than Ronald Reagan was when he became president. Reagan was 69 when he took office. McCain will also become the only president to be born in a U.S. territory outside of the fifty states!

Did you know?
McCain announced that he was running for president in 2008 on the *Late Show with David Letterman*!

Did you know?
As a child, McCain attended about 20 different schools because his father was an admiral in the U.S. Navy.

Did you know?
Senator McCain was born on a naval base in Panama.

Did you know?
John McCain was on the wrestling team in high school.

BARACK OBAMA

Barack Obama is the Democratic candidate. He is a senator from Illinois. Senator Obama's father grew up in Kenya, and his mother grew up in Kansas. Senator Obama has lived all around the world. As a young boy, he lived in Honolulu, Hawaii, and later moved to Indonesia with his family. Obama worked as a lawyer before entering politics. He attended Harvard Law School. If elected, Senator Obama will become the first African-American president in the history of the United States.

Did you know?
Senator Obama played on his high-school varsity basketball team, and still loves shooting hoops in his off-time.

Did you know?
During his time as senator, Obama wrote two best-selling books about his life.

Did you know?
Obama is only the third African-American to be elected to the Senate since the end of Reconstruction.

Did you know?
If Barack Obama wasn't a senator, he would want to be an architect.

AND THE WINNER IS...

Use the stickers to decorate the winner of the election!